The Amazing Life and Loves of Marjorie Fetter Goossens

And the Scandal that Destroyed the Magnificent Career of Eugene A. Goossens III

Glenn N. and Barbara Long Holliman

SUNBURY PRESS

Mechanicsburg, PA USA

Published by Sunbury Press, Inc.
Mechanicsburg, Pennsylvania

SUNBURY
PRESS
www.sunburypress.com

Copyright © 2025 by Glenn N. and Barbara Long Holliman.
Cover Copyright © 2025 by Sunbury Press, Inc.

Sunbury Press supports copyright. Copyright fuels creativity, encourages diverse voices, promotes free speech, and creates a vibrant culture. Thank you for buying an authorized edition of this book and for complying with copyright laws by not reproducing, scanning, or distributing any part of it in any form without permission. You are supporting writers and allowing Sunbury Press to continue to publish books for every reader. For information contact Sunbury Press, Inc., Subsidiary Rights Dept., PO Box 548, Boiling Springs, PA 17007 USA or legal@sunburypress.com.

For information about special discounts for bulk purchases, please contact Sunbury Press Orders Dept. at (855) 338-8359 or orders@sunburypress.com.

To request one of our authors for speaking engagements or book signings, please contact Sunbury Press Publicity Dept. at publicity@sunburypress.com.

FIRST SUNBURY PRESS EDITION: March 2025

Set in Adobe Garamond | Interior design by Crystal Devine | Cover by Victoria Mitchell | Edited by Sarah Peachey.

Publisher's Cataloging-in-Publication Data
Names: Holliman, Glenn N., author | Holliman, Barbara Long, author.
Title: The amazing life and loves of Marjorie Fetter Goossens : and the scandal that destroyed the magnificent career of Eugene A. Goosens III / Glenn N. and Barbara Long Holliman.
Description: First trade paperback edition. | Mechanicsburg, PA : Sunbury Press, 2025.
Summary: This is the story of Lady Marjorie Fetter Goossens, an America woman from rural Central Pennsylvania who found love and meaning amidst an Australian scandal involving her world famous husband, composer and conductor Eugene Goossens III, whose affair with a "witch" rocked the 1950s classical music world.
Identifiers: ISBN 979-8-88819-284-9 (softcover).
Subjects: HISTORY / Australia & New Zealand | MUSIC / Genres & Styles / Classical | BIOGRAPHY & AUTOBIOGRAPHY / Women.

Designed in the USA
0 1 1 2 3 5 8 13 21 34 55

For the Love of Books!

This is dedicated to the independent women
who strive to meet the challenges of life.

CONTENTS

Acknowledgments	vii
Preface	ix

CHAPTERS

1.	Marjorie's Early Life and Loves	1
2.	Third Time a Charm?	12
3.	Ziggy Enters Marjorie's Restless, Reckless Life	27
4.	Separation and Eugene's Knighthood	39
5.	The Conductor's Fatal Attraction	45
6.	The Day the Music Stopped	50
7.	The Aftermath of Scandal	64
8.	The Death of Goossens	75
9.	A Countess Comes to Fetter House	79
10.	After the Storm	87

Epilogue: Finding Alexander, and How the Book Came to Be	94
Endnotes	99
Abbreviations	104
Acknowledgments and Bibliography	105
Index	107
About the Authors	110

Acknowledgments

The authors wish to acknowledge and thank the following for assistance in the preparation of this story: Bobbi Armolt of the Historical Society of Perry County for archival help; Philippe Ballaux for his French hospitality; Gary Eby for Perry County, Pennsylvania, insights; Josephine Field of Normandy, France, for French translations; Grace A. Holliman of Richmond, Virginia for editorial advice, Suzanne Matunis for her Perry County memories of Lady Goossens; Alexander Michalowski of Germany for sharing his family story; Anne M. Taylor for her editorial observations; and Shelia Wayne for shorthand translating skills.

Our thanks to the editorial professionals of Sunbury Press, Sarah Peachey and Crystal Devine, for their numerous skills and patience working with us.

—GNH and BLH

Preface

"All well, ignore press stories"

By cablegram, these five words of bravado were flashed from Australia to France by Sir Eugene A. Goossens III to his wife, Lady Marjorie Fetter Goossens, a few hours after his arrival in Sydney from London on March 9, 1956. Detained by customs agents and interrogated by the police, a firestorm of worldwide publicity brought down Goossens's magnificent classical music conducting and composing career.

The crime for which he pled guilty was that of bringing unlawful pornographic materials into the country, at that time a serious offense. Goossens's situation was complicated by his ongoing affair with the notorious erotic artist and occult devotee Rosaleen Norton, the self-proclaimed witch of Kings Cross, Sydney, a bohemian neighborhood then under the surveillance of the Sydney Police Vice Squad. Only recently invested with a knighthood by Queen Elizabeth II, Goossens went into seclusion, resigned his prestigious classical music positions, and fled Australia two months later under a false name. He never returned, and died a broken man in London six years later.

Thanks to his wife's propensity to save letters, diaries, and memorabilia, historians may now read Goossens's feelings and fears as expressed in his correspondence of that period.

Yet, while Goossens features significantly in this narrative, what follows is Marjorie's remarkable story, a musically talented person born in an era when professional career opportunities for women were limited. This is a tale that involves the lives of prominent, idiosyncratic persons of her time and Marjorie's struggle to understand herself. Let us begin her story in a tiny crossroads village in rural central Pennsylvania.

CHAPTER 1

Marjorie's Early Life and Loves

Growing Up in an Upwardly Mobile, Affluent Family

Marjorie's father, William J. Fetter (1883–1962), descended from a successful first-generation pioneer of Perry County, Pennsylvania, Henry Fetter (1793–1863).

A successful merchant, militia officer, state senator, and farmer, this ancestor erected a stately two-story red brick home in Landisburg with bricks manufactured on site.

Fetter House, Landisburg, Pennsylvania. Authors' Collection.

The 1848 structure, prominently figured in this story, has been called Fetter House since 1974 and is a property of the Historical Society of

Perry County. From 1957 to 1974, Marjorie (1912–2000) made Fetter House her home and eventually left many letters and memorabilia for future historians to discover.

Her third husband, Eugene A. Goossens III, a native of England (1893–1962) and resident of London from 1956 until his death in 1962, visited her only once at Fetter House in August 1961. They agreed to divorce, which never happened due to his subsequent death.

In a strange twist of fate, approximately seven months after Goossens's visit, Marjorie hosted a former lover's pregnant fiancée. A German countess's extensive visit added yet another layer of history to the building's storied past.

In 1914, ambitious William, a mechanically inclined entrepreneur and Lafayette College graduate, moved his wife, Fannie Rhinesmith (1885–1975), and two-year-old daughter, Marjorie, from Alinda, Perry County, Pennsylvania, her birthplace, to the growing city of Carlisle. This relocation over Kittatinny Mountain to Cumberland County was the first of many moves in Marjorie's life.

William and Fannie Rhinesmith Fetter.
MFG Archive.

There, Fetter established an automobile garage and acquired a Buick dealership. Catching the initial wave of the automobile revolution, the family prospered. Marjorie's parents became founders of the local country club and, in the 1940s, purchased a winter home in fashionable Palm Beach, Florida.[1]

The letters of Fannie to her daughter attest to an active social life, suggesting social climbing would not be unknown to Marjorie.

Fetter's Seven Star Garage in Carlisle, Pennsylvania. MFG Archive.

The William Fetter home at 311 S. College Street in Carlisle, Marjorie's childhood home near Dickinson College. MFG Archive.

A second child was born to Fannie and William in 1916, daughter Dorthey Jane. Tragically, Dorthey died of pneumonia in 1921. Marjorie, then age nine, essentially grew up as an only child. Family resources available to Marjorie gave her a financially secure adulthood.[2]

Marjorie, Fannie, and Dorthey, ca. 1918. MFG Archive.

From her father, once featured in the Carlisle newspaper in a community chorus, Marjorie developed a love of music, even singing solo in her local Presbyterian Church at age four.[3]

On Christmas morning in 1927, she received what she later described in her 1969 diary as *"one of the greatest moments of her life,"* a Steinway grand piano. The piano, which can be found in Fetter House today, is still used for musical events.[4]

With growing affluence and perhaps because they were distracted by business and an active social life, her parents sent her at age fourteen to Miss Baldwin's School in Bryn Mawr, Pennsylvania, a posh preparatory institution for young ladies. During her senior year, she participated in the glee club, choir, and orchestra and demonstrated athletic abilities on the hockey and basketball teams. She was also a member of the French club, a language study that was helpful when she made France her home in the 1950s.[5]

Steinway Piano now in Fetter House. MFG Archive.

Marjorie's 1929 yearbook photograph. MFG Archive.

Her scrapbook reveals an active social life attending dances, formal teas, and classical music concerts, a part of her finishing school education that prepared her for upper-class marriages but not a career outside the home. Few professional careers were open to women in the early 1930s, not only due to the Great Depression but to social constraints on women. Such was Marjorie's fate to be born into a generation where she could not use her talents, education, intellect, and personality in employment besides retail, secretarial work, nursing, or teaching. She did, however, make a dazzling celebrity wife, a position she ultimately rejected.

The First Marriage

In 1929, Marjorie enrolled at Bryn Mawr College but later transferred to Mt. Holyoke College. In 1931, she took a semester of classes at the famed Juilliard School of Music in New York City. There, she enrolled in voice and special studies.[6] Again, she transferred colleges in the fall of 1931 to Dickinson in Carlisle.

Art and Marjorie in their few happy days.
MFG Archive.

In 1931, she met Arthur B. Emery, a resident of New York City and a fellow student at Dickinson College. Unbeknownst to her parents, the impetuous young couple eloped in early January 1932.

A marriage announcement appeared two weeks later in the *Carlisle Sentinel*, stating the couple were living at the nineteen-year-old bride's home, as Arthur had taken ill with appendicitis. The youthful marriage ended in divorce in 1935. Marjorie later uncharitably wrote in her 1969 diary of her accountant first husband, "*He was nice, but dull.*"

The Second Marriage

A second marriage followed quickly in June 1936, this time to Philadelphia Main Line attorney John Jacob Foulkrod III, a graduate of prestigious institutions such as the Hill School, Princeton University, and

Dickinson Law School, Carlisle. Engraved invitations were mailed to family and friends, and the wedding occurred in the Fetters' back garden.

One can imagine the bride's mother, Fannie Fetter, was pleased to have a formal ceremony. The groom's parents may have been less happy that their son and heir chose to marry a divorcée.[7]

The couple purchased a house in the Cotswold Village, a fashionable mock English Tudor development in Wynnewood in suburban Philadelphia. They joined with his parents and grandparents, moving in high society as members of the Union Club, the Princeton Club, and the Philadelphia Country Club. The *Philadelphia Inquirer* often mentioned Marjorie's name in its society pages, noting her committee work with the philanthropic charity of Philadelphia's Chamber Orchestra, the Symphonette Society.[8]

The high point of respectable visibility was an *Inquirer* paragraph describing Marjorie at a musical concert in April 1943, looking elegant "*attired in a gray and white smart floral print. Strikingly effective with this was her cardinal red coat with collar and cuffs of soft gray fur. A white camellia, worn on the left lapel, gave a finishing touch.*"[9]

Poised, polished, and well educated in the liberal arts, specifically music, Marjorie moved gracefully in high society living a real-life

John Jacob Foulkrod III, Marjorie's second husband. MFG Archive.

Philadelphia Story in the late 1930s and early 1940s. This was the environment that, a few years later, released Grace Kelly on the silver screen, later the Princess of Monaco. For Marjorie, the girl born in rural Pennsylvania, another step up society's ladder soon beckoned, but not in Philadelphia or Monaco.

During World War II, the year before the flattering article on her fashionable dress, her husband left to join the Army's Judge Advocate General's Corps. After several years stateside, Foulkrod shipped overseas in February 1944 and returned in January 1946.

Marjorie ceased her charity work and, as she wrote decades later, had grown bored with a *Saturday Evening Post*-type life of bridge on Friday nights and John's golf on Saturdays. With a world war on, John was at a distant Army camp, and companies needed workers due to men serving in the military, so she sought work outside of her Wynnewood home.

Perhaps because of her connections to the world of classical music, she took employment with RCA Victor, a major recording and radio company in Camden, New Jersey, just across the Delaware River from Philadelphia. The exact nature of her work is unknown, but after 1943, her name never appeared again in the society pages of Philadelphia.

Separated by months and years of war, many couples who experienced extreme stress and meeting new people found the situation led to the dissolving of marriages. So it was with Marjorie and John Jacob Foulkrod III. Marjorie received a divorce from Reno, Nevada, on December 13, 1945.

Their agreement to part appears to have been mutual as John, in 1947, married a German woman, Irungard Bellingradt, an Allied translator who fled from Nazi Germany to Belgium in 1940. Prior to being a translator, she was a nurse who once spent forty-eight hours buried under a bomb-damaged staircase sheltering two infants. The couple had two children and a successful marriage. Foulkrod passed away in 1979 at age seventy-one.[10]

Marjorie, who saved diaries from 1946 until the early 1970s, kept only three documents from her ten years with Foulkrod: the marriage announcement, a photograph of John, and her divorce decree. Some of what we know of these years is gleaned from newspapers and Carole Rosen's 1993 work, *The Goossens*.[11]

Marjorie's Third Husband, a Famous Classical Conductor

Years later, Eugene A. Goossens III wrote that when he met Marjorie in 1942 while she worked at RCA, he experienced an immediate attraction to the thirty-year-old. Goossens, whose recordings at that time played nationally on leading radio stations, was nineteen years older, a celebrity, and perhaps a quasi-father figure to the much younger woman. Before the year was out, Marjorie visited Eugene, his wife, and two small children in Cincinnati. A few days later, she met John at an Army camp.[12]

A protégé of famed English conductor Sir Thomas Beecham, Eugene and his siblings, all musicians, descended from a line of classical musical conductors. In 1923, Kodak founder George Eastman invited the up-and-coming Goossens to leave London and direct the embryonic Rochester Philharmonic Orchestra and teach at the Eastman School of Music.

A sixty-piece orchestra played in Eastman's "lavishly equipped" 3,500-seat theater. These positions allowed Goossens to travel with his

Eugene A. Goossens, Marjorie's third husband, ca. 1942. MFG Archive.

family to and from London, and guest conduct for orchestras in New York, Philadelphia, San Francisco, Los Angeles, and Boston. These engagements advanced Goossens's reputation.

Born in 1893, Goossens had married English divorcée Dorothy "Boonie" Smith-Dodsworth Millar in 1919. A talented painter with a somewhat Bohemian lifestyle, she came from a wealthy family. Three children emerged from the union: Anne in 1921 and twins Jane and Julia in 1922. The couple divorced in 1928. Boonie had expected Eugene to marry Betty Holmes, a very wealthy widow and supporter of classical music from Cincinnati, who was two decades older than Eugene.

Instead of marrying his "grandmother," as he referred to Holmes, two years after his divorce, Eugene wed one of his American music students, Janet Lewis, fourteen years his junior. They had two daughters, Sidonie, born in 1932, and Renee in 1940. Sidonie was named after her aunt, and

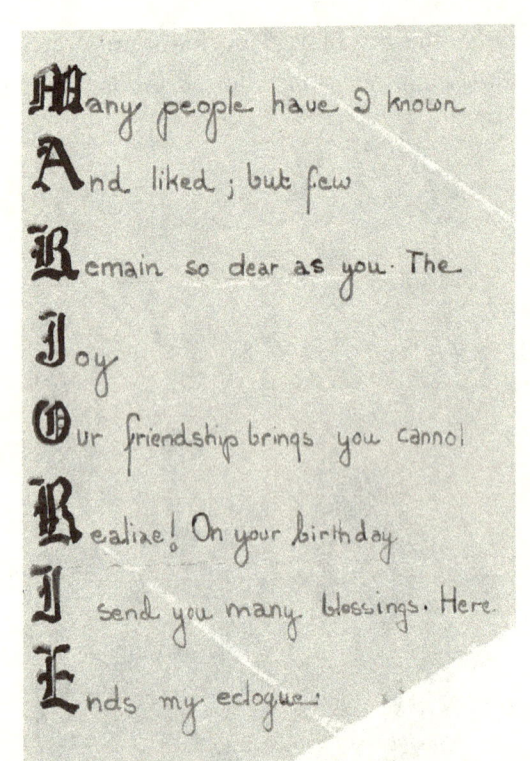

Many people have I known
And liked; but few
Remain so dear as you. The
Joy
Our friendship brings you cannot
Realize! On your birthday
I send you many blessings. Here
Ends my eclogue.

Eugene's letters often had pen and ink drawings demonstrating some artistic ability besides music. MFG Archive.

her family called her "Doni," which she is also called in this book. Renee was not expected. At birth, she was underweight but survived and lived a long but difficult life.

This marriage also resulted in divorce in 1944, clearing the way for Eugene, the conductor of the prestigious Cincinnati Symphony (1931–1946), to exchange vows with Marjorie when she became free to do so. As Eugene wrote of his second wife, *"She over indulged in food, alcohol and men."*[13]

In March 1943, Eugene sent Marjorie an affectionate, hand-drawn birthday card.

Eugene's daughter Doni (1930–2005) remembered Marjorie joining the children with Eugene at least one summer during the war at a guest cottage in Maine. The visit established positive ties between the two females, which lasted until Marjorie's death.[14] Such time evidently cemented a romantic relationship between the two adults.

With the divorce from Foulkrod and exiting her Wynnewood house, she took a flat in New York City, interestingly a floor above the apartment of Janet, Doni, and Renee. Goossens may have made such unusual arrangements so he could see his children and Marjorie during his visits from Ohio. How long this intriguing situation lasted is not known, but both Doni and Renee remembered and remarked on it decades later.

CHAPTER 2

Third Time a Charm?

Marjorie's parents, enjoying the fruits of a successful automobile dealership, had purchased a winter home in Palm Beach, Florida, in the 1940s. Marjorie spent time with her parents in Florida before she boarded a train to Cincinnati in April 1946. That train trip was to initiate her third marriage, this time to Eugene Ansley Goossens III, which would eventually lead her to Australia.

In a letter to his parents in England, whom he had not seen for six years due to World War II, Eugene wrote of Marjorie,

> *She has a fine cultural and musical sensibility – a good pianist (amateur strictly!) . . . She is, in my eyes, a very beautiful and superbly poised woman of the world – a "lady" as we would say in England . . . Above all, she is someone who inspires me to work, who understands me and who has lifted the pall of loneliness which threatened to cloud the rest of my life.*[1]

For their wedding, Eugene and his latest bride slipped out of Cincinnati to avoid publicity, perhaps because his predecessor, Fritz Reine, had his employment cut short in 1931 by the ramifications of divorce and remarriage in a community with a "provincial morality." The groom admonished his latest bride not to dress too stylishly in order to avoid drawing attention from Cincinnati's nationally famous May Festival: "*Eugene said I could not wear the white hat with colored flowers because it was too conspicuous. Since I was also wearing my mink coat and choker pearls, I was hardly inconspicuous!*"[2]

On April 18, 1946, en route to Paris, Kentucky, their car overheated and stalled. After a local farmer filled the radiator, the rescuer followed them to the courthouse to ensure they arrived. Marjorie and Eugene were married in a brief ceremony by a local judge. It was not until May 13 that the *Cincinnati Post* screamed a front-page headline over a huge photograph of Marjorie: "Goossens Secret Wedding to Gotham Woman Revealed."[3]

A few days later, they left the Cincinnati Sinton Hotel and trained to Detroit for a festival concert. Also performing was a young conductor who earlier had worked with Eugene, the soon-to-be-famous Leonard Bernstein. Marjorie observed in 1946 that the future celebrity "*Put on a fine show of knowing all and antagonizing the more.*"[4]

After Detroit, it was back to Cincinnati for the annual May Festival, then to New York to board Cunard's *Queen Mary* and sail to England for a previously scheduled three-month concert tour of Australia.

In that first postwar year, the famous vessel still showed signs of wartime troop service and the more recent transportation of English war brides and their babies to new homes in America. The Goossens were assigned a cabin with bunk beds and mattresses of straw and horsehair. In London, they upgraded to the fashionable Savoy Hotel and, from there, visited Eugene's parents and siblings.[5]

The father, Eugene A. Goossens Jr., had scaled the heights of the English musical world, and his children did likewise. Marie, a harpist, played with the London Philharmonic Orchestra. Sidonie, also a harpist, was the first female to play in the London Symphony Orchestra and later the BBC Orchestra. Leon achieved fame as an oboist. One will find his biography in editions of famous English persons.[6]

After four days, the couple flew to Australia. Eugene had been invited by the Australian Broadcasting Corporation to conduct the Sydney Symphony Orchestra and other orchestras during a three-month tour. The trip in 1946 from London to Australia's largest city was not easy—it took five long days by air with numerous stops.

Immediately after the war, Imperial Airways reconfigured Lancaster Bombers as passenger planes, which carried the Goossens much of their way east. There were stops in Italy, Palestine, India, Singapore, and finally Australia, where they were pleasantly welcomed. After 10,600 miles by

A recognition plaque on the former home of the Goossens family in London. https://www.plaquesoflondon.co.uk/locations/goossens-family/

air and only one overnight in their host city, they flew a Douglas DC-3 to Brisbane for a performance and, one imagines, much-needed rest.[7]

Building a World Class Orchestra

After a successful Australian multi-city tour with various orchestras, the Australian Broadcasting Corporation's ambitious general manager, Charles Moses, offered Goossens the dual role of conducting the orchestra and directing the New South Wales Music Conservatory. Moses sought to develop a superior symphony orchestra to help lead "Down Under" Australia out of wartime cultural isolation. The contract contained clauses similar to Eugene's time in Rochester and Cincinnati. The generous salary was £7,000—about £2,000 more than what the Australian prime minister made at the time. In addition, there would be time off annually to return to Europe to conduct other orchestras and visit family.

Now in his fifties, the middle-aged maestro decided to capitalize on this opportunity to "musically educate" Australia (whose population at the time was less than eight million) and build the Sydney Symphony into *"one of the six best orchestras in the world."*[8] He did so in just two years.

The couple returned to Cincinnati in late October 1946 so Eugene could finish his conducting contract in early 1947. With Doni and Renee living with their mother in New York, Eugene and Marjorie planned their return to Australia. As noted, such a journey to and from the United States to Sydney was not done easily in the early post-World War II years.

Getting There is Half the Fun?

On May 12, 1947, the couple embarked on a two-month journey to initiate Eugene's work in Australia. Marjorie kept a diary in which she often wrote about the odyssey, this time leaving by ship from the west coast. The days on a Canadian Pacific train were restful and engaging, passing through the magnificent scenery of the Rockies. Two days later, they arrived in Vancouver and boarded a small cargo ship with decks covered with lumber. The Chinese crew was "*nice,*" although several had been arrested on the previous voyage for opium smuggling.

There were other passengers aboard. The small cabin had crude accommodations with tiny bunks that proved a torture, but the food was edible. The Goossens loaded nineteen bags for the two-month journey.

One might ask, why not sail to England and fly to Sydney as they had the year before? Undoubtedly the need to bring most of their worldly goods with them at a modest price played a part in the decision. Further, it gave Eugene time to write much of his autobiography, *Overtures and Beginnings,* published in 1952. Marjorie spent much of her time reading; Steinbeck's *Cannery Row* was among the works.

Finally, on May 19, 1947, the ship left Vancouver with the whistle making a "*nerve wracking noise.*" The next day there was sunshine—and sunburns after sitting on lumber all day on the deck. The crew banged on the hull, removing rust with blunt instruments—"*noisy.*"

After days of eating, reading, writing, and sleeping, they celebrated Eugene's fifty-fifth birthday on May 26 with fancy hors d'oeuvres and cake. The next morning the couple recuperated from their hangovers. Eleven days out of Canada, they docked in Honolulu. While the ship was restocking, they checked into the deluxe Royal Hawaiian Hotel on Waikiki. They took a room on the beach for $20 a night and meals to be remembered. The next day, back on board their transport ship, another party; and the day after, yet more hangovers.

On June 4, Marjorie wrote: "*Gene looking wonderful and so am I. He is now writing music. We are now feeling the benefit of the trip. I have now narrowed my drinking to a few cocktails before dinner and feeling better for it."*[9]

Some of the crew did not feel they were benefiting from the long days at sea. Several sailors quarreled with their supervisor, and one sailor bashed in his superior's head with a rice bowl. The chief mended, the long days at sea continued, and the heat increased as they passed the equator and International Date Line. Eugene continued to make progress with his book.

On June 10, a cable arrived, asking Eugene to do a concert in Auckland, New Zealand, to which he was delighted to agree (and received $100 for his efforts). They dug his clothes out of the ship's hold only to discover, to their horror, that mildew had set in. Some time was spent to make the long-tailed tuxedo presentable.

On June 18, they arrived in Auckland, the north island, and Marjorie went shopping while Eugene rehearsed the orchestra. So pleased were the authorities that they insisted he stay for another performance. Finally, on July 7, 1947, two months after embarking from Vancouver, they arrived by flying boat from New Zealand to Sydney, where they were joyfully received as celebrities.

In the next few weeks, in a whirlwind of activity, Eugene directed the Sydney Symphony Orchestra for the first time as their new conductor. Marjorie opened a festival for drama and ballet, Eugene an exhibition for textiles and silk, and both attended a reception at Parliament House in Canberra.

Marjorie's luminary status quickly reached astounding heights. Tabloid the *Sun* declared her "probably the personality of 1947" and lavishly described her as tall with "wheaty" brown and luxuriate feather-cut hair. As if she were a Hollywood beauty being screen-tested, the paper recorded in excruciating detail that she had "wide set long grey eyes, a stout, critical nose, and sun crusted skin as clear and smooth as alabaster."[10]

After almost a year of living in Sydney in rented accommodations, Marjorie returned to the States to pick up the children from Janet, who had proved inadequate as a single parent. To a significant degree, Doni and Renee were being raised by the nanny, Dorothy Cubit. Goossens's three children from his first marriage were primarily raised by their mother, Boonie, although his first-born, Anne, had lived for a time with Eugene and Janet in the 1930s.

Marjorie escorted Doni and Renee to Australia on a cargo ship, the *Mangurella*, arriving in Sydney in July 1948. It had been eighteen months since the children had seen their father.

Left to right, Doni, Eugene, Renee and Marjorie docked in Sydney, 1948. Eugene boarded the ship before his family disembarked to pose for the cameras. MGF archive

Doni, Renee, and Marjorie, a day at an Australian beach. MFG Archive.

Decades later, in her 2003 autobiography, Renee described her stepmother as "*glamorous, talented, tall and beautiful.*" However, many of her observations were also scathing, denouncing Marjorie's later moving her from Australia to France and then "*abandoning*" her in what she termed a wretched boarding school.[11]

A 1947 Australian Broadcasting Corporation news article featured a conversation with Marjorie on what it was like to be married to a famous

Photograph saved by Marjorie from a magazine article about the couple in 1947. MFG Archive.

conductor. She expressed positive feelings about their young marriage, how they were well suited, and how they enjoyed life together. Alas, these feelings changed a few years later.[12]

His Work Prospers

Goossens introduced Australian audiences to more than fifty major works that had previously been ignored or considered too challenging. Audience subscriptions soon doubled, and talk began about the construction of a new opera house for the growing popularity of classical music. It was Eugene who first suggested Bennelong Point in Sydney as a suitable location as he pushed the government for a larger symphony hall. A committee eventually was formed, and, a decade after his death, the futuristic opera house opened. Today, at the Sydney Harbor entrance stands the world-famous 1973 version at Bennelong Point, the location Goossens envisioned.

The 1973 Bennelong Point Opera House, the location first suggested by Eugene Goossens. (Photo by Bernard Spragg. NZ from Christchurch, New Zealand - Sydney Australia., CC0, https://commons.wikimedia.org/w/index.php?curid=70521604)

On occasion, Goossens directed the orchestra before over twenty thousand people at open-air concerts. A television documentary decades later termed him a cultural colossus.[13]

AT THE OPERA. The Governor, Sir John Northcott, attended a performance of Eugene Goossens' opera, "Judith," at the Conservatorium. Sitting with him are Mrs. Goossens (left), the assistant to the director of the Conservatorium, Mr. N. L. Salmon, and Elizabeth Northcott.

Marjorie at a concert with Governor Sir John Northcott at the opera Judith *at the Sydney Conservatorium. Clipping in memorabilia papers, MFG Archive.*

Because they were a famous couple, newspapers sought Marjorie's views on the latest fashions. She modeled her stylish continental wardrobe in 1947 for a color spread in *The Australian Womans Weekly.*

After much searching, the Goossens purchased a large house at 28 Burns Road in Wahroonga, a fashionable suburb on Sydney's upper north shore. Marjorie supplied the funds for the down payment for her first permanent residency since leaving Wynnewood in Pennsylvania.

With improvements in airline service and equipment, the couple often traveled overseas, allowing Eugene to conduct for international audiences. In 1949, there was an extended visit by Marjorie, Renee, Doni, and family valet Albert Wargren to Italy while Eugene conducted in other European venues. The visit included time with Eugene's family in England.[14]

Likewise, the family took a second trip to Europe in 1950. Marjorie wrote in a letter about "*my girls who are darlings.*" She stated that at age eighteen, Doni was already an excellent housekeeper. She reported this stepdaughter would be second harpist for the Sydney Orchestra.

> *Renee, age nine, is an unusual little creature, not beautiful but exceptionally attractive and intelligent. She was undisciplined when she came to me, and we were chin to chin for several months, but I spanked and explained and spanked and explained until she understood who wore the pants and now, I could not ask for more in a little girl. Doni is my companion, but Renee is my baby.*
>
> *They consider me their real mother and I don't think I could be more fond of them if they were really mine. Having them has been a great happiness to me, and I don't feel that I have missed anything with not having my own. Although I was never bitter about it, I felt the lack of children in my life and now I am entirely satisfied.*[15]

Marjorie also visited a French Catholic convent for the first time, never dreaming that two decades later another convent would become her permanent European "home." The girls spent several months in school learning French. The family took a villa in Saint-Jean-Cap-Ferrat with author and playwright Somerset Maugham as a neighbor. Eugene and Somerset were old friends, for, in 1922, Eugene had produced a musical score for Maugham's play *East of Suez.*[16]

In Australia, the family lived well and employed a cook, and a valet/assistant for Eugene. During a time of outstanding personal income, Eugene spent money as it came in, failing to save for retirement or a rainy day. Moreover, behind the family facade, tensions between the husband and the younger wife developed.

Marjorie's diaries reveal her to be an intellectual with deep introspective skills. Her love of reading, art, music, and travel helped define her personality. Always reflecting on life, she turned to spirituality during trips to France and, although raised a Protestant, began to explore the Roman Catholic faith. Marjorie was attracted to the Roman Catholic Church, especially after a visit to Pope Pius XII in 1952. Eugene himself was a Roman Catholic.

A photograph of the family taken at the airport in Nice, France, in 1950. Carlisle Sentinel.

Marjorie wrote enthusiastically, almost too much so, of the meeting with the Pope in her diary. Had she met another father figure that she subconsciously sought?

In her diary, Marjorie wrote, "*I know this is the greatest man I have ever met, the gentlest and most powerful. Nothing I have done in years has excited me so. I do not know why. He saw the rosaries in my hand for the girls and blessed them and gave each a medal.*"[17]

Years later, in March 1956 in France, during a pivotal month in her third marriage, she forsook her Protestant background and was confirmed into the Roman Catholic Church. However, in her journey in faith, she also wrestled with her passion for human love and her attraction to and from men. This dualism increasingly shaped fundamental decisions in her life.

She repeatedly wrote in her diary of loneliness and frustrations. When an Australian publisher rejected her musical compositions for children

Marjorie and Eugene visited the Vatican in 1952. MFG Archive.

for being too difficult, she expressed disappointment. She wearied of being Eugene's "secretary" and not having her own talents and interests recognized.

Dissatisfaction within the marriage increased as Eugene worked long hours and then composed in private at his piano in the home music room. The age difference and temperaments began to make a difference.

Biographer Carole Rosen recorded in 1992 interviews with Eugene's daughter Doni that *"Marjorie was something of an intellectual snob who did not suffer fools gladly."*

Marjorie also wrote in her 1969 reminiscences (some of which she must have shared with Doni years earlier) of the scarring death of her younger sister, her mother's favoritism for the lost child, and Marjorie's belief that she was unattractive. She needed constant male admiration to reaffirm her desirability.[18]

One observer of Marjorie's life, writer Anne M. Taylor, hypothesized that Marjorie lacked a father figure in her growing-up years, which contributed to her seeking approval from men. By age fourteen, Marjorie was enrolled in a boarding school, being removed from her parents for months at a time.[19]

Marjorie wrote in 1952, "*I try so hard, but I feel I am not a pleasant person and I don't understand it. I have everything in the world to make me happy and cheerful.*"[20]

The Marriage Falters

Marjorie endangered their marriage in early 1952 while Eugene was conducting orchestras in South Africa, England, and Europe. She launched an affair with a man very different from Eugene and the social world in which she lived in Sydney. His name was Thomas (whose last name she never revealed), an automobile salesman like her father.

Her diary, much of it written in a secretive shorthand, recorded both her attraction to and anxieties with this relationship and others. Her unique shorthand required a specialist to interpret her words, which Marjorie kept secret from the family.[21]

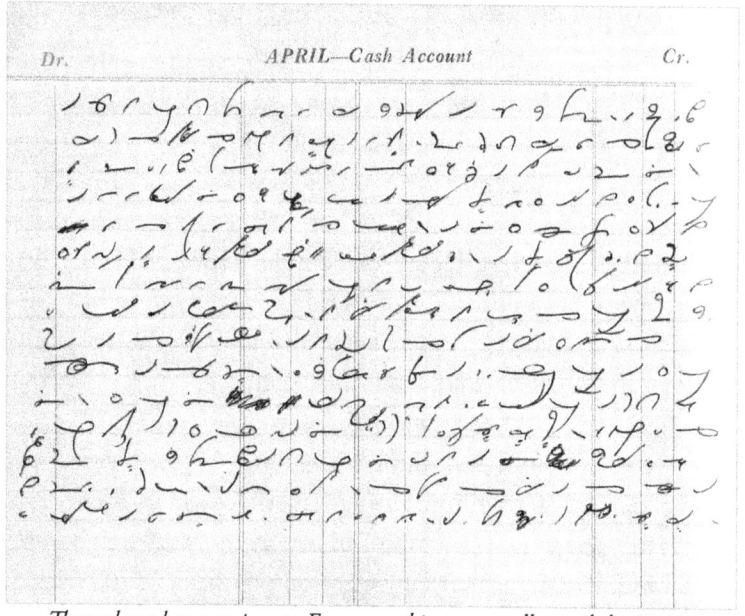

Throughout her marriage to Eugene and intermentally until the 1970s, Marjorie kept a journal, a portion in secret shorthand. MFG Archive.

Another Trip to the States

In April 1952, now involved in the charity the Australian Council for International Societal Services (ACISS) for Displaced Persons from World War II, she flew alone to the States to visit her parents and attend a United Nations migration conference in New York.[22] The family and friends saw her off on a Pan Am flying boat to Hawaii for an extensive five-month visit. She wrote, *"quite numb and cheerful—neither sad nor afraid—only relieved to be off."*

As an adventure, travel was slow by twenty-first-century standards, but the Pan Am service of that pre-jet day was luxurious, with meals shared at tables and private berths for sleeping. There was a day layover in Honolulu, so she went swimming and even surfboarding off Diamond Head. Next, to San Francisco and overnight at the St. Francis Hotel, where she had time for a facial and hair setting before a DC-6 flight to Idlewield (since 1963, named Kennedy), and then local flights to Philadelphia and Harrisburg.

Met by her parents in Carlisle, she felt she had dropped from one lifetime to a past one. After dinner and her first Old Fashioned cocktail in years, she collapsed into a deep sleep. The next day, she shopped in Harrisburg for clothes (*"my first nylon dresses"*), and her father *"gave me such a magnificent present that I can't really believe it. I was flabbergasted! Bless his heart."* This was likely a sizeable sum of money.

After a few days, she took the train to New York City for her conference at the UN, *"devouring the* New York Times*"* en route. She settled in a small suite at the Plaza Hotel for $8 a day. The conference was held at the then new UN building, *"a staggering architectural thing."* Meetings were *"interesting"* although *"not enough resolution copies to go around."* The tables in the cafeteria were closed between 3 and 6 p.m. so that UN delegates *"would not loaf there instead of working."*

There were receptions and dinners to attend. Twice at least she shared a meal and partied with Elizabeth Arden, the cosmetics entrepreneur. Four years later, she would be employed briefly by the Arden company in France. A more jarring dinner conversation was held with a friend from the recording world *"who reported gossip and to find that Janet* [Eugene's second wife] *is spreading dreadful stories about us."*

Marjorie at home in Carlisle with her parents, 1952. MFG Archive.

Marjorie wrote, "*So far have had such an exciting, thrilling time here* [New York], *I don't seem to get tired. So much to do and see and hear. I find life so full and wonderful. Is it just the novelty?—How could I have been so dull and dreary at home* [Australia]. *My poor darling family—how could they have borne with me.*"

Later, after returning to Pennsylvania, she had a reunion lunch in Philadelphia with her second husband, John Foulkrod, at the Princeton Club. "*He seems the same and looks wonderful. He says he is completely satisfied with his life, but I wonder if the 'other road' does not sometime seem nostalgic.*"

In June, she flew to London, had lunch with Eugene's family, attended plays and concerts, and later went to Paris and toured France for a month, sometimes expressing her loneliness in her diary. She became friends with actress Rachel Redgrave, sharing lunch on occasion. In September 1952, she returned to Sydney after five months of travel and decided to break off with her lover, Thomas.[23]

"*From the first of the year, my affair with Thomas, some of it was happy but mostly not. Through the months I was away, I did not hear from him.*" When she came home, she was irritated that he had written her no letters while she was gone. "*I still called Thomas and was desperately unhappy. Really desperately so.*"

On September 23 she wrote, "*I somehow felt our meeting (today) will be the end. It should end, and if only I had the strength I would finish immediately.*"

In her diary, she shared this final statement on October 14, 1952: "*Broke up with Thomas, prayers for good.*"

Unknown to Marjorie, when she wrote this final thought on Thomas, she was about to meet someone who would dramatically change her life.

Eugene Sought Companionship

Also unknown to Marjorie while she was away, Eugene, a successful national celebrity, sought comfort in the company of others. One person in particular captured his attention and would lead to the tragic demise of his career. Her name was Rosaleen Norton, an Australian artist who specialized in occult paintings and claimed to be a witch.

He discovered a book she had written on her art. Eugene, who had an earlier youthful interest in the occult, wrote the author a note of appreciation. Norton, who lived only a five-minute walk from where Eugene worked, invited him to tea, thus beginning a catastrophe for Goossens.[24]

Norton had a placard on the door of her home: "*Welcome to the house of ghosts, goblins, werewolves, vampires, witches, wizards and poltergeist.*"[25]

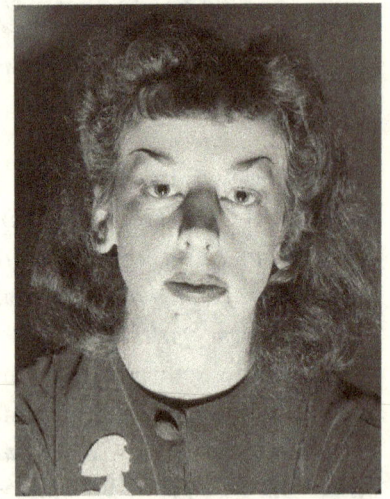

Rosaleen Norton, Kings Cross, Sydney, 21 June 1943, by Ivan, for PIX Magazine, from photographic negative. State Library of New South Wales, ON, 388/Box 020/Item 059.

Unfortunately, Goossens chose to ignore the silliness of the sign and entered into a relationship that would alter the course of his life in a most disastrous way.

CHAPTER 3

Ziggy enters Marjorie's Restless, Reckless Life

The marriage so celebrated in Australian publications moved steadily into uncharted waters in October 1952 when Marjorie had a chance encounter with another representative of ACISS. His name was Zygmunt Antoni Franciszek Kokoszka Michalowski or "Ziggy," an aristocrat with a long lineage of outstanding Polish leaders. As noted by her earlier trip to the United Nations, she served as a volunteer addressing the displaced persons problems of the late war.

The first communication found between the two was a note from Ziggy to Marjorie on November 4, 1952, saying, *"If you come to the meeting, I will sit in a dark corner and admire you."*

Charmed and flattered, she invited Ziggy to dinner at Wahroonga, and he stayed until 4 A.M. He came to dominate Marjorie's heart as no previous or present husband. The attraction was mutual, immediate, and intense. When unable to meet, they telephoned each other regularly

Ziggy, Marjorie's greatest love, was debonair, charming, attracted to women, and committed to freeing Poland from Soviet Communism. MFG Archive.

and wrote numerous letters, which Marjorie saved throughout their deep and long relationship.[1]

She wrote the following in shorthand in her diary on November 13, 1952:

> *Zig broke date due to illness. I find that I have been thinking of him continually and that I am now at the point of being desperately interested in seeing him again. But I am sure that difficulties of that with Thomas affair was nothing but sex or the lack of it. I think it is terribly sad that my life is being ruled by this decision which is really more mental than physical. It is more a need to identify my sex than a craving of body. And I look from man to man hoping that he will be the one who can fill this need which is proved that I did not have with Thomas. I am afraid that this restlessness will ruin me. What can I do?*

Marjorie's feelings quickly led to a physical relationship with Ziggy. After dinner and a ballet on November 18, she found *"him the most exciting lover since Gene."*

Who was this person who so captivated Marjorie's passion?

In 1939, Ziggy escaped the German Nazis invading from the west and the Soviet Union entering Poland from the east. He was imprisoned briefly by the Russians, then, while dodging rifle fire, he and friends crossed the San River into Romania, not yet in the war. He made his way to the British Embassy in Athens and, from there, to France during the "Phony War" of 1939–1940.

After a brief service with the Polish Army in France and as the Germans quickly conquered western Europe by June 1940, Ziggy boarded a ship for England, this time dodging Stuka dive bombers. Ziggy worked for the Polish government in exile and studied law at St. Andrews in Edinburgh and Oxford. With the Soviet Army in charge of Poland after the war, he served as an attaché for the Polish government in exile, this time in Belgium. By 1950, he was helping fellow refugees settle in Australia, an underpopulated continent that welcomed displaced Europeans.

Ziggy descended from a distinguished lineage of wealthy ancestors who, for generations, had served the Habsburg Empire and later the Polish Republic. His father, also named Zygmunt (1881–1947), was

This photograph was taken before the war in the summer of 1939. The location is Stratyn, the estate of family friend Stas Krasicki, in northwest Ukraine. Weeks later, Ziggy, a law student, fled from Poland. Young Ziggy is holding the sun chair. Note his white shoes. The young man with the black hair is his friend Xavery Krasicki. Captured during the conflict, the Russians imprisoned him in a labor camp for the war's duration. He came home after the war "a skull." Knocking on the door of his family's Warsaw apartment, they could not recognize him. Courtesy of Alexander Michalowski, Ziggy's son.

a diplomat who, in 1914, took an assignment as a code translator at the Hapsburg embassy in Belgrade, Serbia. From there, the ambassador delivered the infamous sixteen points to the Serbian government that ignited World War I. With the collapse of the Hapsburg Empire in 1919 and the establishment of the Polish Republic, Zygmunt Senior served for years as the Polish ambassador to Norway, Denmark, and Austria.

Ziggy's mother, Maria Czarnomska Wodzicka Michalowski (1885–1979), wrote an unpublished memoir of childhood, *Memories of Heaven and Hell*, in the 1950s. She described her summer visits to her grandparents' massive estate in Galicia near Podolia, a territory often disputed by the Hapsburg Empire, Poland, and Russia.

The family winter home was in Kraków, Poland. After the collapse of Soviet control in the early 1990s, Ziggy returned to Kraków to live out his days in an apartment in the former family home. Reflecting a changed world, a McDonald's abutted the building.

Six years Marjorie's junior, Ziggy spoke at least four languages, exuded *savoir-faire*, and had a robust personality. Immensely attractive to women, he, in turn, was attracted to the fair sex, even, reports his son Alexander, to the end of his long life (1918–2010). "*My father wore elevated shoes, hated sports, but was charming and made people laugh. He was playful, spontaneous and an original thinker. He was a student of law and philosophy.*"[2]

Ziggy's families lost their fortunes and palatial heritage homes in Poland, what is now western Ukraine, during two world wars and the Soviet takeover of Poland in 1945. After the Second World War, as an exile, he lived on a tight budget while working for international charities. In 1954, he gained employment with Radio Free Europe and rose in the ranks to the directorship of the Polish Department. It was he who arranged for famous Soviet dissident Aleksandr Solzhenitsyn to broadcast his experiences and writings on the radio to Eastern Europe in the 1970s.

Ziggy, born into a Europe devasted by war and political unrest, devoted his life and career to helping restore democratic order and liberty to his Polish homeland. After the collapse of the Soviet Empire in 1990, he received an award from the new pro-Western Polish government for his contributions to the cause of liberty during the Cold War.[3]

Marjorie's Reckless Escape

The communications beginning in November 1952 indicate that Marjorie and Ziggy had strong personalities with definite opinions and expectations of each other.

Amazingly, within two weeks of the November 10 dinner hosted by Marjorie, the two had a tiff. Ziggy apologized in a November 28 telegram. From the first, Marjorie placed demands on his time, wanting them to be together often, and he pleaded that, given his poor financial circumstances, he must work and put in long hours.

This is often a classic conflict in many relationships—career versus time with family, in this case, one person, a demanding Marjorie. This issue remained a stressful point and eventually drove them in different directions.

Perhaps because of their strong egos and passionate natures, their attraction to each other accelerated rapidly.

In her diary on New Year's Eve 1952, she wrote in shorthand, "*This is a lasting love and I am happy.*" A few days later she confided, "*This is the sixth time I have wanted to leave Gene. . . . I am bored.*" Marjorie's infatuation accelerated, and she began moving toward a major decision in her life.

Marjorie may have been unfulfilled in her marriage, but she was often in the society and fashion columns of the Sun *(January 4, 1953) and* Sydney Morning Herald. *She abandoned this exalted position in Australian society for the love of a man, not her husband.*

Ziggy soon received notification for reassignment to Paris. On January 3 and 4, she added to her diary, "*We go for a drive and almost fight. Then . . . we away perhaps in March, I tell my plans to go away . . . I love him and I am attracted too much to him . . . Completely in love and both of us deliriously happy. More discussion of our house in Paris. . . .*"

Her work with ACISS continued, although her thoughts of leaving Australia and Eugene began to jell. In April, she was still volunteering with ACISS as chair of the Integration Committee, the agency she had represented at the United Nations in 1952. The purpose of the charity was to ease the entrance of European intellectuals, doctors, dentists, and scholars into Australian life and to overcome bars to employment. The *Telegraph* reported her as saying, "Australia is wasting a great deal of talent, intelligence, and experience in 'These People.' Why can't we use [them] to our advantage."

The paper also reported Marjorie had just donated office furniture and paintings to the organization. In disposing of the personal paintings, one suspects she was downsizing, preparing for a trip only two months later.[4]

Distressed and madly in love, Marjorie arranged to travel to Europe with Ziggy, not informing Eugene or anyone else of her lover being on the passenger manifest of the Italian liner *Lloyd Triestino*. Her family and friends even saw her off at the Sydney dock on May 30, 1953. Ziggy's son states that his family tradition, confirmed by her diary, is that Ziggy ran off secretly with Marjorie.

Marjorie's excuse for the trip was to rent a house in London for her and her parents during a long visit in the early fall of 1953. After all, she had traveled alone in 1952 for an extended five-month visit in part to see her parents, so perhaps this absence did not seem so peculiar. However, this time her diary knew she had a superseding agenda.

Eugene seems to have made no objections to her departure, evidently moving deeper into his mysterious occult relationships and, according to some accounts, other brief affairs. Over twelve months would pass before Marjorie returned to Australia. By all measures, this reckless action and subsequent disappearance from Australian society endangered her marriage and threatened her reputation in certain circles.

The two lovers had separate quarters for the multiweek cruise to England but were rarely apart. According to Marjorie's confidential shorthand in her diary, their time together became an extended, passionate honeymoon.

Her depth of passion is revealed in the secret shorthand of her diary.

Friday, May 29, 1953

A lovely sail [away] *but I was in a daze. Dinner with the family then to the boat. Phyllis, Bruno, Tana, Prokop, Aileen to see me off, and C. Danes to introduce me to the captain.*

Zig tried to be clever and would not go through the officials with the [result] *that they came into the cabin looking for him. . . . Still do not know if my friends know he is on board.*

Zig came in and we fell on each other's necks but almost [missed] *the entire dinner* [and] *what was going on. Captain wonderful and quickly bought just mine // we leave //.*

Next day, I felt a relationship and had had a glorious day with Zig for the lunch with the delicious wine and food and then two between dinner and the same for Saturday and Sunday. So much in love and so much driving each to be [in] *each other's arms that although it is so marvelously fast, it* [is] *also fun and spirit*[ed] *and mine too. . . . These days much the same, yet sleep and making love. Zig is price*[less] *for me in this way, and we were able to give so much pleasure to each other that is hard not to be in . . . all the time! We are desperately in love, and he is wonderful to me. Kind, thoughtful and xxxxxxx to an imagination with him. I am so happy that it does not seem possible, and he feels the same. I am so grateful for this beautiful experience which is xxx the last of this sort. How we will be able to continue together, I do not know.*

Monday, June 1, 1953

Cause I would never leave Gene permanently, but I do think it will work out well.

Tuesday, June 2, 1953

The day of the Reckoning and we had drinks before dinner and then in the evening a bottle of champagne and were probably drunk! We sat on the floor of my cabin eating biscuits with the wine and were ridiculously happy and gay. What a pleasing after that unhappy affair with Thomas.

This 1953 version of *The Love Boat* ended approximately five weeks later; Ziggy to Paris and work, and she to London to await her parents' visit. William and Fannie Fetter stayed for a month at Marjorie's rented home, 7 Loundes Place in Belgravia.

Her stepdaughter Doni, with whom Marjorie kept a positive relationship her whole life, had written during the summer from Australia that there were rumors she and Eugene would divorce, that Marjorie had been seen often with Ziggy, and there was even talk that he left Australia at the same time she did. In closing her letter, unaware of Marjorie's commitment to a new life, Doni wished her an enjoyable time in Paris.

Ziggy, still on a modest budget, rented an inexpensive room in a Parisian boardinghouse. When not together, they exchanged daily letters and telephoned. Marjorie complained he did not have enough time for her, a theme she expressed often in the next few years. Supportive of him in numerous ways, he thanked her for sending a package to his elderly mother, Maria, in Poland, who fell that autumn and broke her ribs.

7 Loundes Place in Belgravia, 2019. Photo by BLH.

Ziggy wrote in September:

I think of you all the time, when I hear a Citron hooting, I think about concerts. I am seeking work and in a fight for my existence. Must finish this brochure if I hope to get a job. Everyone in Poland [his family] *knows I have been traveling across oceans and continents to see a girl. People in my flat can listen to our calls. It is torture not to be able to say things.*

Her passport reveals three extended trips to the Continent to visit Ziggy in France and Germany in 1953 and 1954. On one occasion, Ziggy met her on the wharf in Dieppe, France. The letters reflect a besotted couple torn between responsibilities and bemoaning their love-struck situation.

Meetings between the couple became more complicated in November 1953. Eugene, on an extended trip to Europe, as allowed by his contract, arrived for several months of concerts playing for the London Symphony and Royal Philharmonic Orchestras. His presence reduced Marjorie's ability to see Ziggy as she attended social events with Eugene and hosted events at her home, but the letters continued.

Marjorie was caught between two worlds and found herself maintaining the facade of the "devoted couple." For the first time in years, Eugene and Marjorie spent Christmas and New Year's with his siblings and father.

Eugene grew ill on this trip, and Marjorie had to refuse invitations and cancel parties on his behalf. The *Sun Herald* of Sydney recorded in February 1954 that Goossens would return to Australia by air and Marjorie by ship. She would bring back "our car" and a four-month-old dachshund puppy she named Bozo.

Eugene returned to Australia in March 1954, evidently recovered from the unknown illness but foreshadowing future health issues. Marjorie stayed in London until July 1954 before traveling to Sydney for Doni's wedding. The puppy is never again mentioned but was photographed professionally with a supposedly happy couple in 1954.[5]

Margorie and Eugene. MFG Archive.

Ziggy's economic situation improved when employed by Radio Free Europe in April 1954, a few months before Marjorie temporarily returned to Australia to attend Doni's wedding. On his identity card, he is listed as a stateless person.

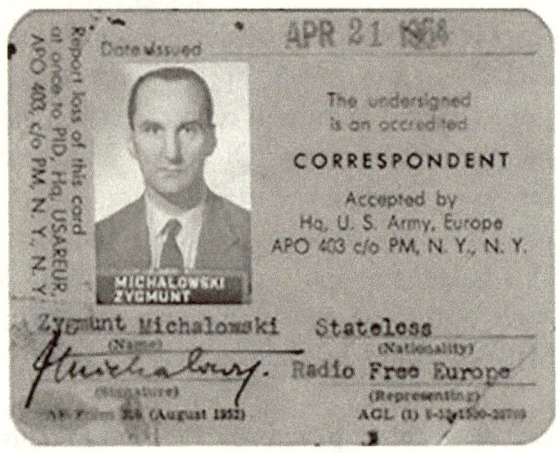

Artifact picture from 1954. Courtesy of Alexander Michalowski.

As Marjorie flipped her life upside down and left her elevated social status position in Australia, she expected much of Ziggy's attention. For example, Marjorie wrote on one occasion about her disappointment in not seeing him at an event. He wrote back that he had to work and was not at her disposal. This exchange of feelings and Ziggy's candid response would be echoed in numerous letters in the next few years. Ziggy could be blunt, perhaps the father figure Marjorie may have desired, expressing himself forcefully when critiquing her temperament and life goals. On occasion, as the years passed, he reduced her to tears. Marjorie sought marriage, but Ziggy did not.

One year into their relationship, on November 20, 1953, in increasing exasperation, he wrote:

You refuse to face the situation you describe as a broken relationship with EG. Your facilitation makes you unhappy and [is] *largely responsible for your nervous irritability. You can only help yourself. Leave EG to worry about things. FIND SOMETHING TO DO WITH YOURSELF. Be a volunteer as you were at the Australian Institute of Social Service.*

In another undated letter, he wrote that he was concerned about her migraines and then went further and expressed some harsh opinions, which are paraphrased here.

- Eugene is successful in Australia, you are jealous of the attention he receives and believe your future bleak in Australia.
- You feel you can't hold your own with other girls and are not pretty.
- You say I don't love you, being selfish thinking of your age and beauty.
- You feel you are not useful.
- If you had to earn a living, you would not worry so much.
- Do not think of noble, all-embracing ideals, causes, and beliefs as a solution for everything.
- Accept life as it is.

Finally – Your migraines may be due to drinks!

Several years passed before their physical and romantic attraction lessened, and, in spite of her demanding his attention and him continuously stating he had to work and not having the financial resources she had, their relationship matured into a lasting, supportive, somewhat unique friendship.[6] In time Marjorie would find something to do besides pining for marriage and a domestic life. However, it would take more years and further education to find a career, such as it was, besides that of church service.

Marjorie's Unhappy Temporary Return to Australia

In the spring of 1954, Doni, a harpist in Sydney, announced her engagement to fellow musical student John Young. A wedding was planned for September 18, 1954. She wrote, asking her stepmother to return for the event, which is puzzling. Marjorie had been quoted in a February newspaper that she would be returning to Australia by ship after Eugene had returned from London by air. Marjorie agreed to attend the marriage and arrived back by ship in early July after over twelve months abroad.

The 1954 wedding took place in the Goossens' garden in Wahroonga. Beginning on the far left stood fourteen-year-old Renee, best man Richard Tiley, Doni and John, Marjorie and Eugene, prim and proper and, one might observe, patrician. MFG Archive.

Behind this facade of a united family stirred the reality of Marjorie's unhappiness in Australia and her immediate desire to return to Europe and Ziggy. She left for England by ship with Renee in early December 1954, using the excuse that the younger stepdaughter would benefit from a European education.

CHAPTER 4

Separation and Eugene's Knighthood

Decades later, in her autobiography, *Belonging*, Renee wrote bitterly of her removal from Australia, believing she was her stepmother's alibi for leaving her father. She described a scene when her father acquiesced almost silently to the decision, bowing to Marjorie's persistence.[1]

Why was Eugene agreeable to this arrangement for Renee? We can project several reasons. With Doni married and Marjorie out of the house, combined with his busy concert and teaching schedule, he would be responsible for supervising Renee. Although he had five children, being a nurturing father never was his strength.

For Renee, the vacancy of Doni from the Wahroonga home and the estranged marriage of her father and stepmother devastated her life.

For Eugene, using the excuse of Renee's education in England would provide needed cover for Marjorie's leaving the family yet again. As noted, Marjorie had been away for five months in 1952 and over thirteen months from May 1953 to July 1954. Renee had to navigate these early adolescent years without the steady presence of an adult female. One could argue Marjorie had become but a shadow in Renee's young life.

Curiously, an announcement appeared in the November 25, 1954, edition of the *Sydney Morning News*, stating that Marjorie and Renee would leave in early December from Melbourne on the ship *Port Townsend* for England. Renee would go to an English school with Eugene's brother's daughter, Connie Goossens. Marjorie would remain in Europe until Eugene arrived in mid-summer of 1955. Then Marjorie visited her family in America, whom she had not seen in years. In truth, her parents had visited London in the autumn of 1953, and she was with them in Pennsylvania in 1952. The mid-summer statement of Eugene's reunion with his wife was in error, as Eugene did not arrive in England to "reunite" with Marjorie until late October 1955.

This article, most likely instigated by Eugene, may have been to forestall talk of divorce in what was still a conservative moral environment in Australia. No doubt Eugene remembered how his predecessor in Cincinnati had lost his position as symphony conductor due to a divorce.

We now know his relationship with occult artist Rosaleen Norton and her followers, although a secret to his family and the public, had deepened, filling his need for companionship.

There was yet another reason unknown to Marjorie. Eugene had befriended Pamela Main, an eighteen-year-old music student of his. Flattered by the attention from the world-famous conductor, their relationship, regardless of the tremendous age difference, became close, parental but with affection.[2]

In early December 1954, Marjorie and Renee boarded the ship and sailed to England. One wonders what of her possessions Marjorie took with her, for she never returned to her Australian home. Obviously she took her diaries, memorabilia, and the letters she had saved.

While at sea, Eugene posted a letter, dated January 8, 1955, to Marjorie that offers insight into the frayed and open marriage. While full of love for her, he also expressed angry recriminations against Marjorie accusing him of an earlier affair.

He also remonstrated:

Yet with only 2 days after your return on the Sibongo [the ship that carried Marjorie back for Doni's wedding in July 1954], *you issued a flat ultimatum of your almost immediate return to Europe. How could it appear otherwise that you sought added justifications for the sudden departure. Your unchanging avoidance of any tenderness in word or action has conveyed too clearly that since your return you did not wish it otherwise. I surmise someone else monopolizes that side of you. Your friendships are your affair short of affecting my dignity or my work.*[3]

After arriving in England on January 19, 1955, Marjorie deposited Renee with Eugene's brother, Leon, and sister-in-law, Ann, and enrolled her in an English school. The relatives evidently felt put upon for the responsibility of caring for Renee. They sent her to Paris. During this second extended trip to Europe, Marjorie took an apartment of wealthy Carlisle, Pennsylvania, friends at 25 rue Dolent, 14th Arrondissement in Paris. There, Renee was encamped temporarily.[4]

Renee's Distress

In April 1955, in what appears to be a selfish act, Marjorie, according to Renee, literally dropped off the adolescent outside of Paris in an austere Dominican school, The Fountains, run by strict nuns. Perhaps Marjorie remembered her own boarding school days with fondness and truly believed this was a good experience for Renee. Perhaps, but probably not. It's more likely that she wanted to live freely with Ziggy, and that was not possible with Renee in the apartment.

Suffering cultural shock and homesickness for her Australian friends and family, Renee became ill and was hospitalized. Doctors suspected appendicitis, but the event, described in Eugene's letters and Renee's bitter autobiography, appears to be the nervous breakdown of a scared, lonely, deserted fifteen-year-old. No physical illness was ever diagnosed.

To add a further negative evaluation of Marjorie's behavior at the onset of the illness, attempts were made to contact her, but she was away in Spain with Ziggy and left no forwarding address. Nor had contact information been left concerning Eugene. Finally tracked down through the passport office, Marjorie broke off her "vacation" with Ziggy and returned to Paris.

Later that summer, she enrolled Renee in a more caring environment, the Convent of the Epiphany, Soisy-sur-Seine, a Roman Catholic convent and school east of Paris. Marjorie retained her separation from Renee but visited her on occasion.

There, Renee recovered emotionally and flourished with kindly nuns and priest/therapist Reverend Dr. John Thompson, who was granted guardianship of Renee. Marjorie acquiesced to this seemingly unusual arrangement as French law required the guardian or parent to be resident

Convent of the Epiphany at Soisy-sur-Seine.

in France. This guardianship would continue until Renee became eighteen years of age.[5]

Renee later moved to Oxford, England, with Dr. Thompson, finished her schooling, and married young. In 1961, she suffered a serious automobile accident, which resulted in a lengthy hospital convalescence and a lifetime of acute pain. In the mid-1960s, divorced a second time, Renee took her son from her second marriage to Australia and made it home for much of her life.[6]

For Marjorie, she struggled with her own feelings. Attraction to both Roman Catholicism and Ziggy conflicted her. It would take until 1957, at age forty-five, for her to make fundamental decisions about the direction of her life.

Goossens receives a Scare and Royal Recognition

While Renee suffered anguish in France, Eugene had his own issues in Australia, including his health and career. In 1953, he had fallen and crushed a vertebra, which required a month's hospitalization. In March 1955, while conducting, he collapsed and was hospitalized, perhaps from dehydration, although possibly something more serious, such as a small stroke. Extensive newspaper reporting on his health demonstrated the esteem he held in the public mind as a highly respected artist.[7]

Reinforcing his position at the summit of Australian society was the private notification in May 1955 that he would be receiving a British

Marjorie in France with her car, the only photograph available of her during her time in Europe from 1953 to 1957. She would take the automobile by ship to Pennsylvania when she returned to the States in the spring of 1957. MFG Archive.

knighthood for his work with the Sydney Orchestra. He wrote Marjorie the good news but asked her not to mention the appointment until it was officially announced in June. Her reaction to this honor is not recorded, as we have few of her letters. However, it could only have been positive as she referred to herself as Lady Goossens for the rest of her life.[8]

On June 8, 1955, the front pages of Australian newspapers announced his Knighthood Bachelor, a KB, along with nine other Australians. Now the title "Sir" replaced "Mr." in front of his name. The next day's edition of the *Sydney Morning Herald* carried an opinion piece that further celebrated the achievements of Goossens, describing him as the "*Master of Our Music*" and "*to hope for a long time to come Sydney will continue to hear his voice in all her music.*"[9]

The paper also explained that Marjorie's continued absence from Australia was "*to be in attendance to their daughter Renee,*" who attended school in France. Further, the paper reported that in July, Lady Goossens would spend a brief time in Pennsylvania and then return to London "*to settle into a home in time for her husband's arrival early in October, and his subsequent five months' concert tour of England and Europe."* There was no home in London as Marjorie continued to make her home in Paris. Eugene made the Colonnade Hotel his domicile while in England, and it appears Marjorie spent time with him on occasion.

Elated, Eugene telephoned her in Paris to confirm the *"elevation to the peerage,"* that he had received 115 telegraphs so far, and public reaction was fantastic. He boasted, *"Apparently no knighthood has ever been so popular."*

While Eugene enjoyed the fame of knighthood, he and Marjorie exchanged letters concerning Renee's situation and health. Not being able, most probably unwilling, to assist his daughter, he wrote in July that he wished he *"could take Renee off your hands."*

He also revealed his view of their estranged marriage, using pleading words. *"You are on my mind eternally. Do you miss me? Want me back? Say you do. Your absence deprives me of a fundamental urge to create."* Yet we know, at this time, he remained involved with Rosaleen Norton. The five-month concert tour in Europe beckoned, and perhaps he hoped for some type of reconciliation.

The Apocalypse by Eugene Goossens

As Eugene's career was about to come tumbling down, it is ironic that while on leave in London in November 1955, he conducted one of his own compositions. This major piece, *The Apocalypse*, is his musical reflection on the New Testament's book of Revelation, which describes the end of time. Ironically, the work foreshadowed the catastrophe that was about to befall him. He had begun composing his oratorio in Cincinnati in 1940 with the assistance of an Episcopal priest who provided notes on the controversial last book in the Christian Bible.[10]

In Sydney the year before, Eugene received a standing ovation when first presented, and over time critics have both praised and panned the work. The symphony is a lavish interpretation of the struggles between good and evil, leading to the last days of Earth before its destruction and the eventual return of Christ. Featured are bombastic drums and wailing horns, signifying conflict, and a massive choir offering words, sometimes hardly understood, as narrative and interpretation.

CHAPTER 5

The Conductor's Fatal Attraction

Eugene's involvement with the "mystical sex magic" of Rosaleen Norton's coven is thought by one observer to have been a late inspiration, at least in part, for his completion of *The Apocalypse*. As a metaphor for the destruction of Goossens's stellar career, the thesis resonates. His sister Sidonie Goossens-Millar observed: "*When he was 11 years old, he was doing etchings which were quite beautiful. Little caricatures and things. He always loved to draw pictures with gargoyles. He had a sort of mania about gargoyles.*"

For example, in the 1920s, he was friends with Cyril Scott, author of *An Outline of Modern Occultism*, and composer Philip Heseltine, who used "Peter Warlock" for his occult musical *nom de plume*.[1]

Rosaleen Norton, an avant-garde painter and worshiper of the god Pan, ran a "coven" from her disheveled home in King's Cross, a bohemian neighborhood in Sydney's red-light district. Eugene joined her coven and participated in "Sex Magic" with Rosaleen, her partner Gavin Greenlees, and others.

Countdown to Destruction

The five months between Eugene's extensive sojourn in Europe before returning to Australia was not a sabbatical but a series of concerts. The press reported a seemingly continuous number of public performances. We can trace his movements by the newspaper reports of those few months before he executed a self-inflicted wound on his career and personal life.

He and Marjorie must have spent time together, as there are no recorded communications from Eugene to his wife from October 1955 until March 9, 1956, a fatal day in the esteemed conductor's career.

October 1955

The headline and story in the *Sydney Morning Herald* of September 30, 1955, announced "*GOOSSENS'S LAST 1955 CONCERT, Sir Eugene Goossens will make his final appearance this season with the Sydney Symphony Orchestra at a subscription concert on October 11—the day before his departure for Britain.*"

Unbeknownst to all, this would be his last public performance in Australia and the last time he met with his orchestra.

The relationship with Rosaleen Norton had been discovered by ambitious tabloid newspaper reporter Joe Morris of the Sydney *Sun*. With radical political beliefs for the time, Norton had come to the attention of the vice police during an era of fear of communism and homosexuality. As if in a *noir* movie, Morris discovered a packet of sexually explicit letters from Eugene to Rosaleen. These were found behind her couch, letters Eugene had asked her to destroy.

By writing letters to Rosaleen, Goossens demonstrated an atrocious lapse of judgment. He remained blissfully unaware that a Sydney vice squad investigation into the mysterious and, at that time, illegal sexual activities of Norton and close friends had been launched. He flew as scheduled on October 12, 1955, to London to conduct, record, and receive his knighthood from the Queen. The investigation continued while he was gone, closing in on his activities.[2]

Goossens resided much of his time in London at the Colonnade Hotel, which was his refuge a year later when his world fell apart in Australia.

How much time he and Marjorie spent together that late fall of 1955 and winter of 1956 cannot be known, although his sister Sidonie reported visiting them both on the night before he began his return to Sydney.[3]

"Sir E. Goossens Wins Laurels in London", *The Age*, Melbourne, October 20, 1955

He received praise when, only having completed the long airplane trip from Australia a week earlier, he replaced his aged mentor Thomas Beecham at a major London performance. In 1923, young Eugene had substituted for Beecham at a Beecham Opera House concert. October 19, 1955, the substitution was for the Royal Symphony Orchestra's opening of its 144th season.

"Panning" For Sir Eugene, *The Age,* Melbourne, October 30, 1955

However, the acclaim for at least one performance turned sour with a damaging review by the *Times* of London for a late October BBC presentation of his oratorio, *The Apocalypse.* The unnamed reviewer from England's most prestigious newspaper labeled the work as *"undistinguished"* and *"tasteless."* Whatever disappointment Eugene felt by this scathing review, and it must have been considerable, feelings were quickly assuaged.

November 1955: The Pinnacle

The Queen Holds Investiture
At Buckingham Palace today the Queen held the first of five investitures arranged for November and December. She bestowed the accolade on five new knights including Sir Eugene Goossens, honored for his services to music in Australia. The Age, Melbourne, November 2, 1955

On November 1, 1955, Eugene reached the height of career success when he received a knighthood from Queen Elizabeth II. Certainly, Marjorie would have accompanied him to the ceremony. Only four months remained before Eugene tumbled from this exalted pinnacle of success.

On November 10, 1955, he conducted in Bournemouth on the east coast of England. Later that month, Eugene fulfilled scheduled obligations in Spain.

How much were the estranged couple together that winter? One hint was a clipping published November 22, 1955, in the *Sydney Morning Herald* announcing that Marjorie had flown to Spain to join Eugene, who directed concerts in Madrid. Both planned to spend Christmas in

Paris with Renee—or so reported the newspapers. The facade of a happy family prevailed in the press.

December 1955

Eugene did take time to pose for a photograph with his father and siblings which appeared in the *London Sunday Times* in early December 1955. The copy read, *"Few stars in the musical firmament shine more brightly than the members of the Goossens Family."*[4]

Although he squeezed in visits with family members, these five months did not involve rest but rather days of rehearsals and numerous presentations, such as conducting the London Symphony on December 11, 1955. He sent a congratulatory cablegram to Australian prime minister Robert Menzies on his reelection that month. The week before Christmas, he conducted for the Society for the Promotion of New Music in London's Festival Hall, as reported in the *London Telegraph*.

Of course, each performance required rehearsals, and such was the frequency that one marvels at Goossens's punishing schedule. Could fatigue have perhaps affected his judgment, leading to the catastrophe that was about to occur?

January 1956

One wonders how long, if at all, Goossens visited Renee in Paris over Christmas. On January 3, 1956, he conducted live a first performance of a work by Denis Aplvor at the London BBC studios, Maida Vale. When did he rehearse with the Royal Philharmonic for this live broadcast?

Still fulfilling public obligations, he spoke on January 16 to the distinguished Composers' Concourse. At the end of the month, he appeared on a live television program with his siblings.[5]

February 1956

His furious pace of travel, practices, and performances climaxed with visits to Hamburg and Vienna. The last half month of leave seems to have been a modest reduction of public appointments and appearances. With some time now for himself, perhaps he then purchased the sexual photographs and paraphernalia, an action, when discovered, that collapsed his career.

A reporter from a London newspaper, spurred on by the Sydney *Sun*, followed some of his movements that month. By the time Goossens boarded his aircraft back to Australia, a trap had been laid and soon would be sprung on the unsuspecting, remarkedly naive conductor.

The *Sydney Morning Herald* announced his March 9 return to Australia. The police and customs officials now knew when he would be returning. Eventually, Eugene walked into their waiting arms.

CHAPTER 6

The Day the Music Stopped

On March 7, 1956, Sir Eugene Goossens, the renowned director of the New South Wales State Conservancy and conductor of the Sydney Symphony Orchestra, boarded a Qantas Super Constellation at London's Heathrow Airport to return to Australia. He had been abroad, knighted by the Queen, highly acclaimed, and applauded for almost five months.

During his time in England, Spain, and several other countries, he conducted symphonies, lectured and broadcast on radio and television, frequented the Savage Club in London (a meeting place for musicians and artists), visited his musically talented father and siblings, and spent time with his wife, Lady Marjorie Fetter Goossens, who lived a separate life in Paris.

On this sojourn in England, he acquired over one thousand photographs—more than eight hundred of which were deemed pornographic—eight erotic books, several ritual masks, and one lewd movie film. He carefully dispersed the items throughout six large pieces of luggage and one briefcase. Some of the materials he meticulously sealed in envelopes with tape and labels with the names of famous composers.

Thirty-six hours later, at Sydney's Mascot Airport, police detective Bert Trevenar, vice squad head Ron Walton, and customs official Inspector Nathanial Craig met Sir Goossens as he disembarked from his noisy four-engine propeller plane (no doubt which made sleeping difficult and Goossens fatigued after his travel). Eugene stepped off the airplane and into his own nightmare, and the prevailing morality of Australian culture and laws of that time.

At age sixty-two, Goossens's hair was receding, mostly white, and combed away from his face. His prominent nose was sharp, the skin above his eyelids was thinning, and his chin was sagging. Evidently, however, his libido remained intact.

No doubt Goossens experienced surprise when Inspector Craig requested to examine his luggage. On his many trips over the past decade from Europe to Australia, Eugene had never been subjected to a baggage check from customs. Exhausted from the travel from England, Eugene reluctantly complied. Taken to a room in the international arrivals shed, inspectors searched his luggage and exposed the contents of the sealed envelopes.

Craig charged Sir Goossens with violating Section 233 of the Customs Act, which prohibits *"the possession or importation of blasphemous, indecent or obscene works or articles."*

For the past six months, Detective Trevenar had been carefully working on a case in Sydney's "red light district" of Kings Cross. Letters and photographs taken from the residence of Rosaleen Norton, also known as "The Witch of Kings Cross," gave police enough evidence to charge Goossens with the "abominable crime of buggery." This law declared sodomy illegal and, if found guilty, carried a fourteen-year prison term. Fortunately for Goossens, higher authorities chose not to charge the more serious violation, reducing his embarrassment and any potential imprisonment.

This was fortunate since *Sun* reporter Joe Morris had infiltrated the coven and found the letters Eugene foolishly had written to Rosaleen, which she had hidden behind her couch. They were suppressed at the time but were made public years later. One by Goossens read: *"I need your physical presence very much, for many reasons. We have many rituals and indulgences to undertake. And I want to take more photos."*

These letters clearly indicated that Goossens participated in the practice of Pantheism and resultant sexual activity with Norton and her homosexual boyfriend, Gavin Greenlees.[1]

Vice Squad seized Goossens's pictures
Vice squad police stopped world-famous conductor Sir Eugene Goosens when he flew into Mascot Airport today. They seized eight hundred photographs and films from his luggage. Then Sir Eugene was taken to

police headquarters. He stayed seven hours. "It was a friendly chat," he said when he left.
—*Sydney Morning Herald*, March 10, 1956

Over the decades, the public story of Eugene's detainment on March 9, 1956, his court hearing, and subsequent resignation from the Sydney Symphony Orchestra and director of the New South Wales Music Conservancy has been covered in numerous articles and books.

Goossens's Tragic Communications with Marjorie

However, for the first time for publication, we now know the raw, personal feelings Goossens experienced between his arrest and flight from Australia two months later. Marjorie saved his numerous cablegrams and the letters he sent to her in Paris. Eventually the material made its way to Fetter House in Landisburg, Pennsylvania.

Eugene's first cablegram was sent on March 9, the day of his detainment. "*All well, ignore press stories.*"

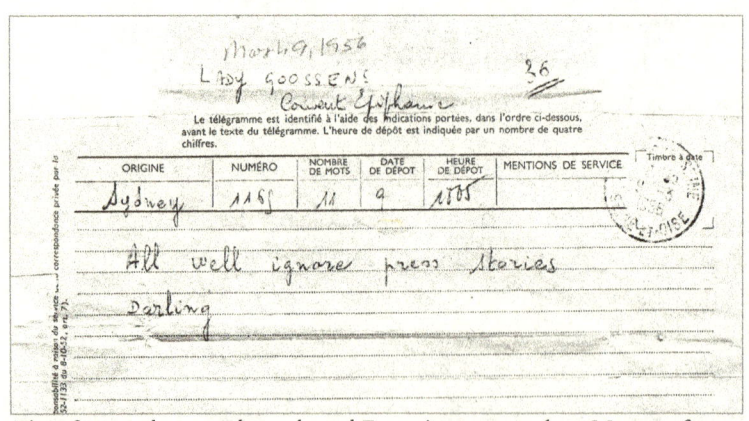

These five words express bravado and Eugene's attempt to keep Marjorie from forming an opinion based on the lurid reporting that exploded in the world press the next day.

The news of the disaster reached her in France when the *Sun* made telephone contact. Marjorie denied rumors of a separation and stated she would stand by her husband and return to Sydney the moment he needed her. None of this would prove true.

Three days later, Goossens sent his second cable, poorly punctuated, to Marjorie. *"Written fully advisable stay there darling pending outcome favorable developments appearances misleading and suspend judgement cabling westminster contrite love."*

A damaged front page of the Sun *found in Marjorie's Pennsylvania memorabilia. We can only speculate on how she obtained it. As it had been folded, it may have been mailed to her from an Australian acquaintance. MFG Archive.*

Breaking down this message, he advised her not to come to be with him, as the press had asked if she would do so. *"Favorable developments"* is bluster, and *"appearances misleading"* is the first indication of his creating a story to cover his embarrassment. *"Cabling westminster"* may have been an early attempt to ensure his knighthood would not be revoked. The word *"contrite"* may be his feeling of desperation and increasing depression at his situation.

A March 14, 1956, cablegram to Marjorie with original punctuation read, "*Blessings inspiring sun interview Health splendid Vidication later pray always devotedly.*"

Goossens was responding to a *Sun* article that quoted Marjorie. He stated his health was splendid, yet he gave ill health as an excuse for taking a leave of absence from his positions and to appear in court with his attorney. "*Vidication later*" is preparing her for his description of the incident. "*Pray always*" is evidence of his latent Roman Catholic faith re-emerging during his horrible crisis.

The next day, he cabled, "*Reported you plan instant return fearful affect nervous strain of immediate situation on your health suggest later return by boat but will welcome and abide by any other decision you make love always.*" The thought that he would lose his position or leave Australia evidently had not yet crossed his mind.

At the magistrate court hearing on March 22, Goossens reportedly was still too ill to appear. On behalf of his client, attorney Jack Shand pled guilty. The guilty plea ensured there was no lascivious display of the "exhibits." On the facts, particularly the conductor's admissions at Mascot, there seemed no practical defense. He was fined £100.

"Goossens 'Guilty' Plea to Customs Charge: Fined" screamed a headline in a *Sydney Morning Herald* paper.[2] This was followed up by a March 22, 1956, cablegram to Marjorie: "*Fine insignificant compared with dangerous threats which compelled my action All well love.*"

Goossens had constructed an excuse for his actions. He began to spin a tale of what is likely a wild, pathetic fabrication. The imaginative mind of Goossens, which allowed him to create musical stories, worked overtime as he strained to create a plausible excuse for his actions.

The fine of £100 levied by the court dealt only with bringing banned materials into Australia. The additional issue of his involvement with Norton's coven was not introduced nor mentioned in the press until sometime in the future. Evidently his wife did not, at that time, know of Rosaleen Norton.

Goossen's letters to Rosaleen Norton were not submitted in evidence during the trial. Authorities hushed up his relationship with her coven and other prominent persons.

With the trial behind him, he received his first letter from Marjorie, one that provided some solace. No letters from Marjorie to Eugene were in her memorabilia, although in 1957 she saved a copy of a bitter letter to her husband, never wishing to see him again.

March 23, 1956, Eugene's letter to Marjorie
My own adored one,

Your dear charitable generous letter came to me this morning, the morning after the hearing before the magistrate. You know now of the fine, which there was no hope of escaping, [irrespective] of my motive for bringing in what I did bring. (In my next letter, in a couple of days, I will detail the matter; you will then know of the fear motive back of the whole thing, a feature which was brought out by my lawyer, and duly emphasised by the press. . . . This helped to confirm in most people's minds what they suspected from the first, that I was acting under duress. I hope this element was referenced to in the European papers. It should help to exculpate me).

I did not attend the hearings yesterday, a doctor's certificate sparing me that final ordeal; the increasing strain and tension of the past fortnight has taken its toll in nervous exhaustion and physical fatigue, though, thank God, I am surprisingly well on the whole. So that had I been compelled yesterday to face again the barrage of flash bulbs, reporters, as [well as] *the whole set-up of legal machinery in a courtroom, I could not have borne it. There are limits to stoicism.*

Fortunately, the magistrate and counsel kept things to a minimum. This was essential not to rake up unnecessary detail. Both my solicitor and Shand, Q.C. were excellent in this respect. Moses, I am told, created a tremendous impression.

I say "I am told" because since that first awful day of my arrival, I have lacked [the] *courage to read a single newspaper and have relied on a rough idea of their contents on Doni here at 28* [his home]. *Her cheerfulness and amazing calm in coping with telephones, press calls, etc., has been of enormous help to me, and you would have been proud of her.*

It is yet too soon, my Darling, to arrive at a definitive decision as to the future. My revulsion to the whole atmosphere is, as one can guess, all too vivid, as my desire to be rid of this country, as to seek the calm and refuge of Europe and you have been the uppermost thought in my mind throughout this whole nightmare.

> *In a letter I wrote to Moses this morning thanking him for his support yesterday, I drew his attention to an early decision on the matter. The reaction of the public—now that the case is over—will soon be sensed. Undoubtedly with the A.B.C., as the Con* [Convervancy] *won't waste time inviting my resignation if my continued functioning with both of them is going to prove mutually embarassing. My present association with both of them is temporarily suspended on the grounds of ill health—this arrangement was mutually agreed upon as the only solution to the problem of my conducting the first* [missing word] *and taking Conservatory classes.*
>
> *(I haven't been out of the house for 14 days except to see Greenaway for a medical certificate. If a full resignation from both organizations seems indicated, it will be on the same health grounds.)*
>
> *However, I will be in a better position, my darling, to tell you in a few days what is going to happen. Rest assured, that whatever is decided, will be for the best.*
>
> *Yes, my religion has been an enormous comfort for me during these dark, horrible days. Your new crucifix lives always on my person; God bless you for our faith in me, and charity towards me in the future.*
>
> *Your adoring loyal G.*
>
> *PS—Doni sends her love. Blessings to the sisters at the* [convent]

On March 25, 1956, Eugene sent a cablegram to Marjorie: "*Your dear letter greatest inspiration well love.*" A suffering Eugene was grateful for his estranged wife's support, as his cablegram and remaining letters record during this terrible upheaval in his life.

Unfortunately Eugene did not save letters from Marjorie, nor did she usually make copies. On March 25, 1956, Goossens's English agent, Wilfred Van Wyck, wrote, and Eugene forwarded his letter to Marjorie.

"*My Dear Gene, I want you to know that you are very much in my thoughts these days. It is not too difficult to imagine the agony of pain thru you must be passing . . . you have a loyal, affectionate and steadfast friend on whom you can always rely.*"

Marjorie's mother, Fannie Fetter, wrote from her winter home in Palm Beach, Florida, that month.

Gene's case sounds very grim, too, if he is sick. I feel very sorry for him. Hope you don't go to Australia and get mixed up with it. We have not been called by reporters but the story has been in the papers and quite a lurid one yesterday.

Do you think he is innocent? I am afraid his career is ruined and what will he do? If you sell your property in Sydney, can you get your money out of the place? Have you told Renee the story about Gene? We feel sorry for all of you.[3]

On March 31, 1956, while Eugene suffered his travail, Marjorie took the major step of being baptized and confirmed into the Roman Catholic Church, leaving her Protestant roots behind. Renee witnessed this Easter Saturday service at the Convent of the Epiphany in Soisy-sur-Seine, outside Paris. Marjorie no doubt was comforted by this action. In Australia, Eugene continued to experience emotional devastation as his world continued to collapse around him.

An April 11, 1956, cablegram from Eugene to Marjorie read, "*Resignations accepted; grateful letter, wrote tonight.*" The following letter to Marjorie details his dismissal from his positions:

April 11, 1956
My own Darling,

Your letter arrived this morning—a fateful day, for Moses just called to say the Commission decided to accept my resignation. I can't help feeling some relief about this decision (Incidentally, I cabled you 1/2 hour ago "Resignations accepted, etc") for the newspapers have, as you can imagine, made life such hell and have made it so hard for me to stage a 100% comeback, despite the paradox that in so doing they

Sir Eugene Goossens is fined £80

SYDNEY, Thursday. — Sir Eugene Goossens, world-famous conductor, was fined £A100 (£80 sterling) today for importing indecent articles, books, prints, photographs and films.

Sir Eugene, who pleaded guilty, was not in court. His counsel, Mr. J. W. Shand, QC, produced a medical certificate that he is in "a state of mental and physical collapse."

Sir Eugene is 62. He has been married three times.

Mr. Shand told the court: "These photographs were brought out as the result of the threats of another, the nature of which will become known very soon. The matter is now under investigation."

Clippings found in Marjorie's memorabilia which may have been mailed to her during the crisis. She was receiving information on developments from sources other than Eugene. MFG Archive.

have hardened public opinion almost wholly in my favor, that I am now glad to shake the dust of this ill-starred country from my feet.

Outside of what I have achieved artistically, it has brought me so little happiness or good fortune, and likewise to you, poor darling—that I have countless times regretted our decision to come here. . . . As I told you in my last letter, I shant go into any details (if you want them) until I know all my letters are reaching you unopened. I am so bored and heart sick with the whole thing—which is so complex—that I can easily dispense with the retelling of it again (except to Sidonie in England, I have given no hint to others of what lay behind it). Enough that it has cost me my job—but it's an ill wind, etc. And I am penitent, contrite and have suffered unimaginably!

But now we must get down to realities. I shall telephone Oakes tomorrow and tell him of your wishes about the sale of the house. . . . Shall I dispose of the books in the living room, and in my room at the Con., or should I have them crated and returned to England? To store in England depending on what our plans turn out to be.

Eugene went on to state he would dispose of the two pianos and be content with an upright instrument in the future and that he had nothing of sentimental value in his personal belongings. Legal fees of £566 and the £100 fine, therefore, "*created a hole*" in his bank account. He wrote of following Marjorie's wishes for an inventory of the house, recalled some lent furnishings, and stated she should write Oakes (their real estate agent), giving him the power to dispose of the house. As Marjorie's mother indicated, this letter restates Marjorie's money underwrote the purchase of the house.

In his revealing letter, he further stated the importance of his faith during this painful episode in his life. He chronicled his increasing despair:

Each day is a nightmare, and will continue so until I leave here. But I hate my environment and its population, which brings up the question of my return. It is too soon today, when I have just learnt my fate, to tell you how I shall return. I am strongly tempted to return by ship which would give me 5 or 6 weeks of badly needed recuperative rest.

These angry words about Australia, written on one of the worst days of his life, ignored the successes he had achieved and the admiring press and audiences that celebrated his tenure over the years. Undoubtedly his depression was near overwhelming and he felt the need to strike out at something, somebody, in his embarrassment and despair. Even in the crisis, the *Sydney Morning Herald* wrote generously of his talents and achievements and announced his resignation "*with profound sadness*" and that the end of his Australian career was "*pitiful beyond measure*."[4]

In an April 17, 1956, letter to Marjorie, Eugene, with his "resignations" accepted, begins to make plans to leave Australia for his native country, England:

> *My last messages to you were the cable and letter of the 11th telling you of my resignation being accepted by the ABC. Salmon and many other officials think a terrible mistake was made by the Commission in the acting, and the orchestra and big percentage of the concert public are frankly disgusted. But that's now in the past, as the future alone counts. There isn't a vacant cabin in any boat leaving here for Europe in the next 6 weeks. It's the peak season, so this washes out my idea of a sea trip. Moreover, even if a small freighter or an Italian boat were available, the thought of sitting vis-à-vis with the same 12 people for 6 weeks is stifling. I shall therefore return by air.*
>
> *I <u>will not</u> land at a British airport. The thought and prospect of a horde of pressmen, each one distorting any words of mine and making a world-wide press resurgence with sensational angles descending on at a London airport might precipitate in me a nervous crisis which after all I have gone through (and am still to a lesser degree enduring in my complete isolation) induces in me a nightmare of terrified anticipation. I do not, for obvious psychological reasons and my professional future, want to make a noisy return to my native country.*

Goossens desired to book a flight on KLM, intending to land in Amsterdam and then take the channel ferry to Harwick, England. However, Marjorie insisted on his first resting at a retreat center in southern France for economy's sake. Although independently secure herself, she had been receiving a monthly stipend from him; hence now some need to economize.

Letters crossed in the mail, and in reply on April 18, Eugene wrote

> Your assurances of understanding and loving sympathy are doing wonders in my rehabilitation of morale; the "pariah complex" rubs off when you speak to me. The physical loathing of everything to do with this physical A[ustralian] environment is something I want to soon escape from. I would go tomorrow if there were not things to look after.[5]

Eugene, caught up in an emotional storm, did not note that this was the tenth anniversary of their marriage.

In this letter, Eugene gave details of selling furniture and disposing of books and other items but again reiterated he did not wish to return to England to face reporters and a *"gutter press."*

> I will not be faced by a horrid barrage of press again, anywhere. This is why I don't want you to mention to even my family or anyone the date or place of my return to Europe. This is something you alone must bear the secret of. One leak and my isolation is at an end. . . . Let me know your opinion of a "continental vegetation" period for me.
>
> You may have your own plans and may be bored and adverse to the idea of spending a consecutive number of days or weeks in my company in any place other than our permanent future home. If so I shall understand, darling, and be content to spend that time alone—but <u>not too long</u> apart from it!![6]

Alas, Eugene's dream of reuniting with Marjorie was the opposite of her own desires as soon became evident during their short time together at the Dominican convent at Saint-Mathieu-de-Tréviers near Montpellier, France.

On May 4, 1956, Eugene wrote to Marjorie from Doni's home in Melbourne, a respite good for his emotional condition. The ABC agreed to pay the £400 for Eugene's airfare to Europe. Books and musical materials were to arrive by steamer in crates. Eugene would leave on May 24 for Rome, transferring to Nice, where Marjorie would meet him and take him to the convent.

The next and last letter from Eugene on May 12, 1956, is one he delayed writing but knew he had to do. The lengthy five-page letter is reproduced here. As expressed earlier, this is a fabrication, a creative story to make himself the victim of a tall tale, disregarding his own naivety, sexual passions, and destructive actions. What follows is Eugene's attempt to be persuasive. A follow-up to these accusations never occurred by any legal entity.

My Darling,

I wrote two days ago with final details of arrival at Nice. I take the 10 o'clock Air France plane from Rome on the morning of the 27th, arriving Nice after 11 (I leave here KLM on the 24th).

Some time ago, I told you as soon as I knew my letters were reaching you unopened, I would write you the details of the cause of my misfortune. As you can imagine, Darling, to talk about it or write about it, it's like probing into a wound. But it seems ridiculous that you should not have some data about it before I arrive. You can also imagine that the less I discuss it with you when the blessed time comes when we are together again, how happy I shall be. I want no dark clouds to evolk the immediate, to mar the sunshine of our reunion—except when it becomes absolutely necessary to refer to that immediate past.

<u>But you don't have to read what follows unless you absolutely want to.</u>

I think it was Nov. 4th last when I received a telephone call at Maida Vale BBC studios (I write all this from memory but I think it was before an Apocalypse rehearsal and that you were there, and I took the call in the small conductor room). The conversation went something like this—"Can I talk with you privately over the phone, this is a Mr. Parry speaking." I replied that I was at a rehearsal and asked what the matter was about.

"Well, I've to talk with you very confidentially," the voice replied.

It all sounded so serious and a bit alarming that I ended up telling the man to either call me at the hotel or preferably at the Savage Club, where I'd be that afternoon. (Mystery #1 how did he know I was at the BBC that morning?) I rang off and later the call came while I was at the club—that afternoon.

"We want to know when you will be returning to Australia," he started quite bruskly. I told him and later "We want you to take something over there with you."

I resented his tone, and when he said what it was he wanted me (or they) to take: "some prohibited photographic stuff" the nature of which he cruelly hinted at clicked! You can guess, Darling, that by this time, I was getting quite a shock. After I'd given him to understand that he was talking to the wrong person, as that I'd had enough of the conversation, he started off with threats, beginning one about Kings Cross gangs, and how he'd make the Sydney press make it appear I was mixed up with them, and make the papers print a few nice things about "you and your wife's private lives." And more the like, but he left the worst to the end.

"If you don't do what we want, or double cross us, we'll get you and your daughter." He yelled this down the phone. I wasn't afraid of anything they might try as involve us with, so far as gangs were concerned, because I had and still have—a clear record on this score, but I was scared about physical violence on either Doni or me. (I have naturally never told D that she was included in the threats the language used by this man Parry, connected with her, wasn't at all pretty.)

A week or more later, he again rang up—at the Club—and repeated all the above, adding "We'll fix the Customs" (oh yeah!) and telling me at what shop the stuff could be procured. I tried to forget the whole thing, but, as you can imagine, it haunted me; I didn't want to precipitate a nervous "crisis" by telling you (you were none too well, as it was) nor did I dare to take steps for police protection—especially as there [would] have been "publicity" to cope with. And, oh God, what a share of that was to come to me eventually!

Again, in January, the man called me at the Savage (he tried 3 days in succession). I remember the day because I dined with Bill James that night at the I.M.A. Again, just before I left for Vienna, he called, increasingly threatening, and when I told him that I'd bought a small quantity of the stuff, just to see what effect this would have on him, he was derisive and inferred that it'd be the worse for me if I didn't get much more. I asked him what I was to do with what I'd purchased when I got to Australia, he answered "You don't have to worry, *they'll* contact you."

Unfortunately when I got to Sydney, I could [not] and didn't dare to reveal what I was forced to bring what I did. My luggage had never ever been opened on any previous visit to Sydney, ironically! Moreover this, plus the fact that the Sun had its front page virtually set in print before my arrival is set proof that I was deliberately framed.

Even at the Magistrate's hearing, however, my council judged it wise not to stress the circumstances or nature of the threats, because of the extra publicity this would involve and the possibility of a hornet's nest being stirred up in 2 or 3 counties looking for the perpetrators of the scheme. Rivals, obviously, since nothing was gained by my bringing over the packets except my own discredit—except for those who believe in me.

I am tired of writing and re-envolking all of this. The rest, with all its angles and its sunnier side of restoration of confidence over here. We will talk about whenever you are interested.

CHAPTER 7

The Aftermath of Scandal

On May 24, 1956, under the assumed name of Mr. E. Gray and driven to the airport by his son-in-law John Young, Goossens flew the multi-stop flight to Rome from Sydney on his sixty-third birthday. After changing planes in Rome, he landed in Nice, where Marjorie met him. She drove the exhausted Eugene to the convent of Saint-Mathieu-de-Tréviers in southern France. Previously she had attended retreats there and, less than two decades later, would make it her permanent home.[1]

After several weeks, Marjorie left Goossens and traveled to Oxford to check on Renee, who had relocated to school there under the continued legal supervision of Reverend Dr. John Thompson, the psychologist and Roman Catholic priest. In July 1956, Eugene left the convent, returned quietly to England, and boarded temporarily with his siblings.

Goossens escaped Australia, never to return, but his tragedy followed him, virtually destroying what was left of his career. In the summer of 1956, he had no home, no job, and, for the most part, no companionship with his wife.

After several months of living with his siblings, he moved to the Colonnade, lived out of his luggage for months, and wrote letters to Marjorie, full of pathos, begging for her presence and describing how he hoped to restart his work. Here are a few.

On July 12, 1956, Eugene resided temporarily in Lewes, England, at a sibling's home. He wrote to Marjorie in Oxford, England:

My heart is heavy that you are not here . . . do consider 2 or 3 days together before you vanish to France. Moreover, I am not happy at the

> *thought of you burying yourselves* [with Renee] *in Oxford much longer, as also I think psychologically (visions of my Pa and the family) we should find at least a little time together.*
>
> *I shall be glad when August comes so I can go somewhere and deposit my luggage some place for at least a month. Later on I can find myself a couple of furnished rooms somewhere in London rather than doing the rounds of family, which is getting unsettling and demoralizing. Friday last, despite our rather unhappy morning, was a glimpse of you, and I hated letting you go. Just as I hate in so many ways you taking a distant job, you are most keen on. I suppose it is one of my punishments and real anguishes is the thought of constant separations from you.*

His asking Majorie to return permanently continued for several years. "*Do you miss me? Do you want me back? Say you do. Your absence deprives me of the fundamental urge to create as it has since 1942. My happiness is still and always centered in you.*"

She did rejoin him temporarily in the late summer of 1956 at the London Colonnade, residing in separate rooms.[2]

After a visit to Pennsylvania, Marjorie returned to Paris, taking a position in sales at Elizabeth Arden, the cosmetics company located in Place Vendôme. This unusual act evidently was to replace the loss of monthly financial support Eugene had given her for several years. It was her first job since her wartime employment at RCA Victor in New Jersey. She did not find satisfaction in this work and resigned within six months.

Ziggy, who continued to write regularly and, ever the realist, wrote, "*are you sure this job, plus your religious extravagancies, do not tire you physically with having to get up at 6 a.m. and stand up all day?*"[3]

Her Anger at Eugene Continued

In her memorabilia, Marjorie left a draft copy of a bitter letter she wrote to Eugene in February 1957.

> *You may remember after the Australian scandal I would not stand with you or put up with anymore nonsense from you if you did not break off completely what ever you had been doing in Sydney. I do not want to*

have anything more to do with you now nor do I intend to see you either in Paris or elsewhere. First I can't help you, or change your image and I do not wish to be involved again by you in another scandal.[4]

Even after this letter, Eugene delusionally continued to pursue her. He rented a London flat at 76 Hamilton Terrace, leaving his room at the Colonnade Hotel. Eugene sent Marjorie a diagram of his apartment, even designating her room. Goossens put his fantasy on cardboard, which Marjorie saved.

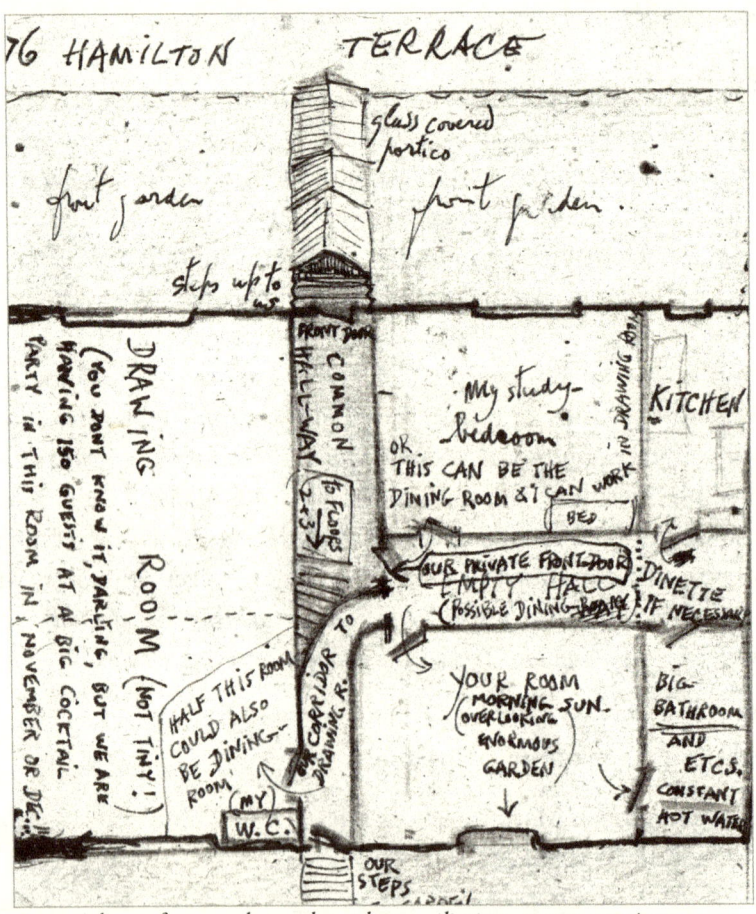

Eugene's letters for several years begged reconciliation, even to creating a drawing of his flat, including Marjorie's proposed room. The comparison of his accommodations compared to their former Australian home is startling and emblematic of Eugene's career collapse. MFG Archive.

Yet, while seeking his wife's return, Eugene was inviting Pamela Main, his much younger Australian friend, to move to London and reside with him as his housekeeper and secretarial assistant before he vacated the Colonnade Hotel. Eventually, Pamela, who would inherit his royalties, migrated to England and cared for him for his last years. One wonders at Eugene's continuing enticements for Marjorie to return as he also welcomed Pamela's attention. Undoubtedly, he was lonely, depressed, and craving companionship and affection.[5]

Yet Another Man in Marjorie's Life

As if life was not complicated and stressful enough for Marjorie, in the fall of 1956, she became enamored with a former British Army colonel, Christopher "Kit," or "K," Blauth, who lived and worked in London as an insurance executive. For six months his letters were ardent, although he had a wife and two sons. In the winter of 1957, reflecting a growing sense of frustration and evident confusion, she wrote Ziggy, in essence demanding him to "*Move to Pennsylvania and live with me or I will marry the Colonel.*"[6]

Ruling out marriage with Marjorie, Ziggy, always candidly observant, responded:

> *I accept the fact you run from one thing to another, selling and renting houses and cars for no obvious purpose, going to parties and then having headaches. You would be bored living with me working ten hours a day and having veal cutlets for dinner on my poor pay. You would just have more of your hysterical scenes and frequent migraines.*[7]

In her journal, she recorded a frenzied, frantic period in her life. She saw Eugene on January 30, 1957, Kit on February 1, Ziggy on February 6, and Kit again on February 9 and 10, February 16 and 17, and March 2, 3, 9, and 10. During this hectic period, Renee visited her in April. Marjorie also traveled to Spain and back to France.[8]

Marjorie Made a Decision

Four years after fleeing Australia and Eugene, Marjorie arrived at a decision point in her life. In the spring of 1957, she recognized her marriage to Goossens was over except for a divorce. Marriage to Ziggy appeared out of the question. Christopher, a family man, younger and passionately in love with her, was not a suitable option.

Noting her indecision and confused thinking, Ziggy sternly wrote:

Do you indeed think of changing from being Catholic to something else being under the impression that you will then be allowed to have four living husbands? You now may want to throw your faith overboard so that you won't be lonely in old age? Really, coming from you this is quite out of order! I wish you were here. I NEED TO TALK TO YOU![9]

The issues in Marjorie's life cascaded—relationships with men, dissatisfaction with her work, disgust with Eugene, and, four years since leaving Australia, the lack of a "*home*" and focus.

I am desperately lonely. I realize it is too late for me to have what I have always wanted, a happy home with a husband who is just that in every sense of the word. It is impossible for me to face the rest of my life wandering back and forth around the world with no purpose. I'm not made that way.[10]

Fetter House, the family's ancestral home in Pennsylvania, now appeared as a solace for the wandering Marjorie. Her father, having recently inherited the Landisburg home, agreed for her to make it her home, although he had doubts that, after cosmopolitan Europe, she would be comfortable living in an American rural environment.

With this opportunity, Marjorie left her employment, male friends, marriage, and any supervision of Renee and returned to the community of her birth, Perry County, Pennsylvania. There, in a quiet, bucolic setting, she would rest and sort out her thinking.

In May 1957, she sailed from Italy to the States with fifteen boxes and her luggage, among which had to be the saved letters from the three men then in her life. While the 1848 Fetter House was being renovated, Marjorie lived in the Mill Apartments on Carlisle Pike near Harrisburg. Upon reflection, she made another transforming decision at the age of forty-five: to pursue the study of medieval music, particularly Gregorian chant, reflecting her interest in traditional Catholic rituals.[11]

Marjorie, an Excellent Student

She embarked in four years of study, first at Mary Manse College in Toledo, Ohio, studying Gregorian chant. She then enrolled as a resident student and graduated with honors and a master's degree in music from the University of Indiana Jacob's School of Music in January 1962. For these degrees, both *summa cum laude*, she both resided on campus and took correspondence courses. This period was probably when her grand piano moved from her parents' home in Carlisle to Fetter House, where it resides today. One can imagine her utilizing it in her studies.[12]

An informal photograph of a relaxed and happy Marjorie, but loneliness was never far away. MFG Archive.

Yet even with the heavy educational demands and residential attendance on campuses, she found time to visit Europe in 1959 and several times for extended periods with her parents in Palm Beach. Ziggy, remaining a close but no longer romantic friend, visited her at Fetter

House in 1958. He had to testify in support of Radio Free Europe before a congressional committee in Washington, D.C. Another visit to Landisburg occurred in 1960. They corresponded monthly, and she always saw him when visiting Europe.[13]

Return to Europe

Ever the traveler, she broke off her studies in the spring of 1959 to return to Europe, rediscovering the cultural atmosphere where she increasingly felt most comfortable. The voyage to Italy also awakened some feelings she had tried to suppress.

Below are her diary entries from her time traveling to Italy on the *Saturnia*.

February 18, 1959: " *am so lonely.*"

February 20: "*To NY, bitter cold. Dinner with John* [Thompson]. *He said Renee was in a pre-schizophrenic stage and I could have done nothing—bad sleep, depressed.*"

February 21: "*Mass and confession. Go to the docks. Given me a good room. During take-off, I put clothes away, baggage was lost. Wonderful to hear Italian and French. Savored lunch and wine and walked in sun. Lovely sea. Roses from G.* [Goossens]. *Bless him. Dinner is a shock, very nice Canadians, better than US who would be a strain.*"

February 22: "*Tired, weather rough. Cocktails with my Canadian tablemates who are very nice.*"

February 23: "*Mass on ship, Asian rite, very different. Still rough and cold, stayed on deck most of day.*"

February 24: "*Same indefinite number of days feeling very alone, but health better, walked a lot although weather bad. Hesitate to put down my weaknesses, my delight to have attention again* [from a man], *from first day of boat drill where I thought him so very handsome in that finely drawn Italian aristocratic way, and then he turned out to be one—in the reading room, walking on the deck, every time we met a recognition.* [She goes on about this married man.] *I write with shame. He is a* *jet pilot on the NATO station missile project in the US. I, utter bitch that I am, am fascinated into moral immobility. I know it is wrong, yet my susceptibility is so strong that it terrifies me—loneliness, time of life, whatever—I pray to be delivered from the body of these depths. But I think it is over anyway, and he has given me a happy few days of feeling in contact with someone like him—he knew I watched when they left the ship, and from far off waved to me. When we walked the day before he talked of me with complete understanding, and when his family did not meet him, he told me his disappointment. So far so very good, better no more. Atmosphere* [was] *as if I had never been away for two years!"*

Ever the Italian tourist, she visited Venice, Florence, and Rome, stayed with the daughter and son-in-law (the Crosses) of novelist Robert Graves, and lunched twice with English poet and playwright Christopher Fry, whom she liked *"immediately and enormously."*

She met Ziggy in Paris several times for dinner, and things did not go well, as they bickered almost like an old married couple. There was an exchange of letters, curt and aggravating. Each time, Marjorie wrote she would not contact him again. There were tears and half-reconciliation.

Separate visits to the Soisy-sur-Seine convent proved comforting. She wrote when there that she was *"at home."*

Marjorie spent two weeks in England, remarkedly half the time at Eugene's flat. He met her at the station *"with a mustache, posture worse and thin and nervous. The atmosphere* [was] *as if I had never been away* [she had not seen him since January 1957]. *Apartment lovely but filthy, no place to hang clothes or put things. Dinner in SoHo, much to talk about. Decided G. never changes because façade always the same."*

During her time at his flat, she tried to have serious conversations and asked if he wanted a divorce. *"He denies everything of course; also got off my chest about his hobbies which he also denies. Not much use talking to him."* The word "hobbies" referred to Marjorie's euphemism for diverse sexual activities.

Eugene met her at Southampton and took her to dinner as she prepared to take the channel ferry to France. *"I am enormously relieved to be leaving him and his flat; the effort to meet his false intimacy is tiring. I weep bitterly to see any past hopes turned into a seedy, apologetic, rather furtive old* man. *His kindness makes it even harder, and his attempt at sentimentality force a travesty and reminder of how much I loved him. I feel I won't see him again.*"[14]

Eugene, on the other hand, was still extravagant in words and unrealistic in his estimation of their relationship. He wrote her a letter after the meeting, their first time together in over two and a half years.

"*We had such a ridiculous evening in our search for a Dover Sole and the always and unbreakable feeling of oneness which both of us felt so inevitably—I think you felt it, as did I that furtive tear in your eye at our parting was an indication. You are my only beloved and I worship you utterly and belong to you.*"[15]

She returned to the convent in Soisy-sur-Seine, foreshadowing a future life in a French convent environment with nuns and no men. After four months in Europe, she sailed to the States and resumed her advanced degree in music.[16]

This trip, when she again felt the tug of human passion, resulted in a major decision. As she wrote a few years later, her battle was between human desire for male companionship and religion. God won, she said, and she took vows in later 1959 as a Dominican Nun, 3rd Degree Secular. With this decision, she no longer wrote of conflicted feelings between physical desire and spirituality.[17]

Renee

During her 1959 holiday, Marjorie visited Renee in Oxford for one day and spent time with her in-laws, Leon and Sidonie (Eugene's sister) and their spouses. Letters indicate she often corresponded with Renee, Doni, Reverend Dr. John Thompson, an English Gregorian chant expert named A.G. Murray, and friends in New York City and at the University of Indiana.

Marjorie's relationship with Renee appeared positive even providing her stepdaughter with financial aid, but decades later, in her 2003 autobiography, Renee was unsparing in her criticism of her stepmother. She blamed Marjorie for her removal from Australia in 1954 and subsequent abandonment in boarding school environments. Renee had another major reason for growing angry with her stepmother and Eugene.

In Renee's autobiography, she tells of having a 1958 meeting with her natural mother, Janet, whom she had not seen in ten years. At lunch in England on Renee's eighteenth birthday, Janet told her that Goossens was not her biological father. Rather, Renee was the result of a brief affair with a Swedish violinist named Eric during the time Eugene, Janet, and Doni had lived in Cincinnati.

Eugene and his family, including Marjorie, had known of the parentage but had never shared it with Renee, who was devasted by the news. In answering a distraught letter from Renee, Eugene confirmed his ex-wife's statement but said it made no difference to him, that Renee was his daughter, regardless of the lack of a genetic connection.

Belonging, Renee's 2003 autobiography.

In addition to emotional stress, her life was forever changed as a result of a horrible automobile accident with her second husband in 1961. She spent more than a year in an English hospital and sadly coped the rest of her life with pain. In 2001, she published *Pain Management*. According to a January 1, 2001, *Sydney Morning News* report, she lived in England then and wrote articles for *The Disabled Motorist*.

Renee would cling proudly to her Goossens name, but her relationships with the family, including Doni, deteriorated and never reconciled, although the sisters both attended the dedication of the world-famous Sydney Opera House in 1973. An October 21, 1973 article in the *Sydney Herald* identified Doni as Sidonie G. Scott and her sister as Renee G. Moore.[18]

Pamela Main and Eugene

In London, Eugene struggled to earn a living. His agent, Wick, arranged for recording work with the BBC and, when possible, guest-conducting engagements. Goossens directed orchestras in Hungary and Argentina in 1957 and later in Toronto, Canada. Eugene begged Marjorie to join him when in Canada. Pleading a cold, she refused to make the trip from her parents' winter home in January 1958.

After Eugene took the flat in London, Pamela Main left Australia sometime in 1958 and moved in with Eugene, serving as his housekeeper. Whatever their relationship, which she hoped would end in marriage, her presence comforted the older and increasingly sickly Eugene.[19]

Celebrity couple Richard Bonynge and Joan Sutherland visited him at his London flat several times. Bonynge remarked, "*Tragic to see him. It seemed he had become half his size. He was absolutely destroyed physically. I believe Australia destroyed him. Definitely, he was pillared by a very insular society.*"[20]

CHAPTER 8

The Death of Goossens

In the summer of 1961, an increasingly fragile Eugene conducted two concerts in Bear Mountain, New York. The engagements, a week apart, allowed him to travel to Landisburg and make his one and only visit to Fetter House. His purpose was to discuss divorce, an issue he wished to address in person with Marjorie.

Cordially, they agreed to commence the legal procedure with Eugene undertaking arrangements in England. While visiting, he utilized Marjorie's beloved grand piano to perform the Gregorian chant she had written for her master's program. After his overnight visit, he graciously wrote her on August 6, 1961: "*To say I was impressed by your work on Gregorian Chants is putting it mildly. I came away with a strong feeling of inferiority complex about the whole thing! I saw for myself the idyllic place in which you pass most of your days. A breathtaking, beautiful bit of America.*"[1]

But the divorce was not to be. When he returned to England and began working on the legal process, to his amazement, his solicitors notified him that his 1928 Swiss divorce was not recognized by British law. Therefore, Boonie and he were still legally married. He wrote from London that he now had to institute divorce proceedings against his first wife, requiring a trip to Switzerland. With a smile in his writing, he noted: "*After thirty years and two intervening wives thrown in, this might have entertainment value for a theatrical comedy!*"[2]

His Health Collapsed

Pamela Main wrote to Marjorie in January 1962 that Eugene had developed pleurisy and was retaining water. A few weeks later, doctors diagnosed heart failure and stated that he should never conduct again. However, now always in economic stress, he managed winter engagements in Paris and London, conducting from a chair.

Other than conducting, he could no longer care for himself except for eating, tying his tie, and shaving around a beard he had begun growing. The last photographs taken in January vividly show his declining physical health.

Pamela sent this photograph to Marjorie in January 1962. MFG Archive.

Pamela wrote of the constant care she was giving him, even installing an electric bell in his room to ring her during the night. Ill health postponed the necessary trip to Switzerland until June, and then, with deep concerns, Pamela escorted him to Geneva, where they stayed at a pension and spent time with his twin daughters, Jane and Julia, from his first and apparently still-legal marriage.

Eugene wrote a final letter to Marjorie, thanking her for allowing him to charge her with desertion in the divorce suit. He also revealed he had £350 and owed Inland Revenue £300, making him a pauper.

In a letter written to Marjorie the day after Eugene's death, Pamela wrote he had been wheelchair-bound, ate two prunes, said, "*I feel sick,*" and began vomiting blood. Taken to a Swiss hospital and drugged into unconsciousness, he received "*pints of blood but the shock of losing so much was too much for his heart.*"

With airplane reservations already made for a return to London and encouraged to do so by the Swiss physicians, Pamela kept her promise to him to take him home. Daughter Jane accompanied them on the flight, which the captain allowed only after Jane signed a paper of responsibility. Thirty minutes late taking off, the flight seemed endless. Rushed to a London hospital, Jane and Pamela spent the night with him. He was weak and had difficulty breathing. Eugene received the last rites and, the next morning, June 13, 1962, he died. Pamela believed it was cancer, but "*one would never know.*"[3] However, the official cause of death is recorded as a ruptured ulcer.[4]

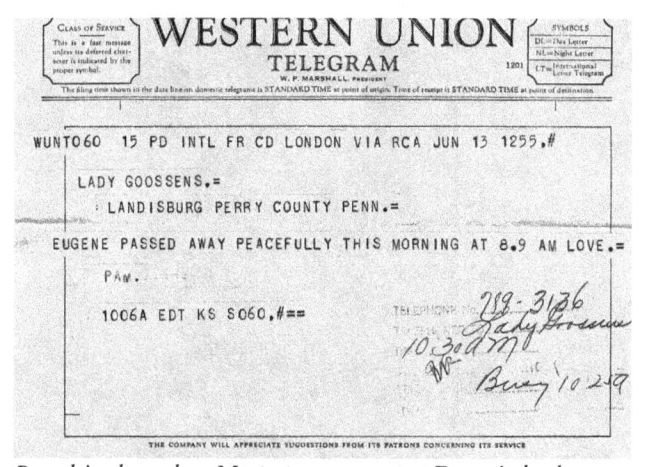

Pamela's telegraph to Marjorie, announcing Eugene's death.
MFG Archive.

Pamela lived briefly with Eugene's sister Sidonie in Surry, and together they settled his affairs. He had earned large sums during his career but saved little. Lavish entertainment, travel, children's schooling, and servant's wages consumed decades of his income.

Pamela received the rights to his music and supervised the copyrights of his recordings and compositions, for the rest of her life. She died in 2005. Eugene is buried in St. Pancras Cemetery at Islington, a London district.[5]

When the iconic Sydney Opera House was dedicated in 1971, Goossens, the conductor who, more than anyone, brought serious music to Australia, was not mentioned.

However, in 1982, at the now world-famous Sydney Opera House, a bust of Goossens's likeness was placed in the concert hall's foyer. The sculpture was created by Peter Latona and paid for by opera house subscribers. In 1991, the Australia Broadcasting Corporation honored Eugene by naming a small concert and recording facility after him at their Ultimo, Sydney, complex.

Photo by Russell Hoover.

Early in the new century, a movie explored the life and artwork of Rosaleen Norton and noted Eugene's involvement in her coven. A few of his Norton letters survived and, along with his life, were reviewed in a radio interview with Renee and Pamela in 2004. The authorities destroyed all other materials associated with the 1956 customs episode.[6]

The sadness of the abrupt ending of Eugene's Australian career lingers in cultural history, but the music he celebrated and the music hall he encouraged live on.

Although an international traveler, Marjorie made no effort to attend his 1962 funeral. That summer of 1962, when Eugene died, her own life was engulfed in the unexpected responsibility of providing hospitality at Fetter House to a wealthy, pregnant European countess.

CHAPTER 9

A Countess Comes to Fetter House

On August 27, 1955, the front page of the *Carlisle Sentinel* read:

Swedish Count
Stockach, Germany – *Count Robert Douglas, a Swedish agricultural expert, who once turned down an appointment by Hitler, died. His age was 75. Count Douglas, whose father was a Swedish Foreign Minister, lived in Germany for many years. He became a German citizen but assumed Swedish nationality again in 1945.*

Just seven years later, in a Carlisle hospital, the only daughter of Count Douglas gave birth to one of his grandsons, Alexander Douglas. He died one of the wealthiest men in Germany and the husband of the widow of the deposed King of Portugal. There was no mention of the mother's exalted social status in the birth announcement because Countess Marie-Louise Douglas Bieberstein, age forty-one, was living incognito at Fetter House in pastoral Perry County with Marjorie.

How did this come to be?

"I am in trouble...," wrote Marjorie's former lover, Ziggy, on November 28, 1961.

> *I am writing you to help me if possible. I am involved with a nice and charming person and are expecting a baby in 7 months. She is in the midst of a divorce taking years. If discovered she is pregnant by German law, this cancels the divorce. We have to hide the fact. This is where you come into the picture. Can she stay at your house? Do you think this is*

reasonable or mad? She has some of her own money and speaks English a little. She needs someone for moral support.[1]

What Ziggy did not mention, and evidently did not have total awareness of, was Marie-Louise also suffered from a serious nervous disposition and hysteria. That Marjorie soon would learn as would Ziggy.

Countess Marie-Louise Douglas, whose smile hid a dangerous condition. MFG Archive.

Marjorie generously opened her expansive American home in 1962 to the distraught Marie-Louise, a refugee from her angry, vindictive, older German husband from whom she sought a difficult divorce.

While sheltering from an Allied air raid during World War II, Marie-Louise met Dennis von Bieberstein-Krasicki, a member of the diplomatic corps who was twenty years her senior. They married in December 1944 at her home, the Langenstein castle at Lake Constance, Germany. During their eighteen years of marriage, there were no children. Alexander, Ziggy's son, the baby to be born in America, further reports the Douglas family did not like the husband.

In 1961, Ziggy met Marie-Louise at a Munich reception, and a relationship developed. Already, she was in the midst of divorce proceedings against Dennis.[2]

Marie-Louise's mother, Sophie Douglas, the first wife of Count Robert Douglas, wrote Marjorie from Constance, beginning a multi-year relationship until the old countess's death in 1971.

Dear Lady Goossens,
 I thank you with all my heart that my dear Marie-Louise may spend these last weeks of a very trying time with you in your home. I have read several of your kind letters to her and feel much better about the whole situation. . . . You certainly know she has an old mother of 76 with heart trouble. We have spent a week together although we have many problems to solve.
 It is certainly quite necessary now for her to leave Europe on account of her divorce. Before she has [the] *child and is married, I believe her husband would try to take up the case again, saying she was divorced on false terms. I pray to God that it be his will that she gets her divorce after these five years. . . . Let me thank you again most heartedly for your kindness to my dear child. May God bless you for this kind deed. I am so glad you will meet my daughter in New York.*
 Yours very sincerely, Sophie Douglas[3]

Arriving seven months pregnant in Pennsylvania in March 1962, Marie-Louise and Marjorie became close. However, soon after arriving, Marie-Louise had a nervous attack that so upset Marjorie that she called the local physician, Dr. Joe Matunis, who administered a calming injection. Ziggy confessed by letter that these attacks had happened before and advised that alcoholic beverages be kept away from her.

On May 31, 1962, Dr. Matunis delivered her child, a boy. She named him Alexander Douglas (her maiden name) as she was not yet divorced from her husband or married to Ziggy. For the baby's first six weeks of his life, he lived with his mother and Marjorie at Fetter House.

In mid-July, Ziggy flew over and joined the now-divorced Marie-Louise in Landisburg. Their marriage took place at the Carlisle registry office, and soon the new family returned to Ziggy's small flat in Munich, Germany.

However, the couple did not live happily ever after. Emotional distress and incompatibility engulfed the couple. Marie-Louise suffered depression, exacerbated by post-partum issues. Ziggy, long a bachelor, proved unsuitable for marriage.

Upon returning to Munich, Ziggy wrote Marjorie, admitting he had made a *"dreadful mistake"* and that Marie-Louise was unstable. A German doctor diagnosed that the baby's health was at risk due to the mother's intermittent breastfeeding. Writing Marjorie herself, Marie-Louise poured out her frustrations and fears, felt she could not cope, and even asked Marjorie if she would adopt Alexander.[4]

Marie-Louise's mother, Countess Sophie Douglas, distraught by the conflict the couple was experiencing, continued to write often to Marjorie, thanking her for taking care of her only daughter.[5]

Sophie descended from American/Scandinavian parents whose relatives were titled and owners of outstanding European properties. Born in Bergen, Norway, she grew up in Seattle, Washington. She met Robert Douglas at the German embassy in Cairo, Egypt, in 1902 on a world tour financed and chaperoned by a wealthy aunt.

The Douglas family was one of the wealthiest in Europe, and Robert held the title of chamberlain to the King of Sweden. After three sons and daughter Marie-Louise, the marriage deteriorated. The couple divorced in 1937, and two years later, Robert married Queen Augusta Victoria, widow of the deposed king of Portugal, Manuel II, and a distant cousin of the exiled Kaiser Frederic Wilhelm II of Germany.

Both parents asked Marjorie to serve as godmother to Alexander, to which Marjorie kindly agreed. Marjorie arrived in France by ship in late August 1962 and traveled to her Paris convent. Unfortunately, before departing for Munich, she received word that her father had become seriously ill. She broke off the trip and immediately returned to Pennsylvania. William Fetter died in December 1962.[6]

Marjorie continued to receive letters in an ongoing three-way relationship with Marie-Louise, Sophie Douglas, and Ziggy, the confidante of all, a sounding board for their frustrations, worries, and anxieties. In one letter, Marie-Louise threatened suicide. Marjorie anxiously pleaded with her not to do something injurious, to think of her newborn son, Alexander.

After several months of mutual misery, and Ziggy nearing his own nervous breakdown, Marie-Louise took the baby to her childhood home in Lake Constance. There, her aged mother helped care for her and

At Villa Douglas at Lake Constance, Germany, the divorced Sophie lived separately from her ex-husband and his second wife. Here, Ziggy's son, Alexander, lived with his maternal grandmother, Sophie, until age six, when he united with his father in Munich. Courtesy of Alexander Michalowski.

Alexander. Ziggy made several driving trips from Munich to Constance to visit his son and check on his wife.

The Death of a Countess

Marie-Louise's mental health grew worse, and, in February 1963, Sophie placed her in a local sanitarium. On April 28, 1963, Marie left her room, climbed the stairs to an unlocked attic door, walked to a window, climbed on a table, threw herself out the now-open window, fell several floors, and impaled herself on a fence. She survived two days. Alexander, her only child, was only eleven months old.[7]

Eugene Goossens, Marie-Louise Douglas Michalowski, and William Fetter all died in the space of nine months, undoubtedly bringing great grief and distress to Marjorie.

Later in the summer of 1963, Ziggy returned to Fetter House, his fourth visit, taking comfort with his best friend, Marjorie. One can hope they found solace in each other's company.[8]

Late in 1963 and early in 1964, Sophie wrote, seeking Marjorie's reflections on the past year of anguish.

> Nach schwerer Krankheit verschied im Alter von 41 Jahren am 29. April
> meine liebe Frau, die Mutter meines Kindes, meine geliebte Tochter,
> unsere Schwester, Schwägerin und Tante
>
> ### Marie-Louise von Michalowski
>
> geb. Gräfin Douglas
>
> Zygmunt von Michalowski
> Alexander von Michalowski
> Gräfin Sophie Douglas
> Graf und Gräfin Wilhelm Douglas
> Graf und Gräfin Ludwig Douglas
> Graf und Gräfin Robert Douglas
>
> München, Kufsteiner Platz 5 · Konstanz (Villa Douglas)
> Schloß Langenstein
>
> Die Beisetzung findet am Freitag, den 3. Mai 1963, 16 Uhr, auf dem Friedhof Konstanz-Allmannsdorf statt.

The funeral card of Marie-Louise. MFG Archive.

On December 6, 1963, Sophie wrote to Marjorie:

If I understand you right, you left Z; you did not want to marry him and in your sorrow and despair you found help in the Catholic religion. It must have been terrible for you to see my darling Lillian [the family name for Marie-Louise] *and her child leave you with Z when you knew he would leave her soon. He told you this! This was too much for her, my poor child, who had suffered so much before this foolishness.*

Z very often told and wrote to Lillian that he was too difficult and was not a man for a married life. Lillian spent months in Munich as his wife, October, November, and December [1962]. *She was very ill and did not understand that she was doomed to die of the shock she got as Z left her in* [unable to decipher word]. *Z was also very nervous, not normal, and Lillian was very unhappy with him.*

On January 1, 1964, Sophie wrote to Marjorie:

I remember she wrote to you and telegraph to you in her despair when Zygmunt left her with the baby. She became a shock of the nerves. A deadly one, the doctors say, and it caused a defect of motion matter [in] *the brain. The last four weeks of her life I shared the room with her; she suffered terribly of a cramp in the brain. She did not lose her mind for a minute, but she suffered so horribly, and the doctors seemed not able to help her. She did not seem to find any way out of her misery. She was utterly unhappy that she was not allowed to see her beloved child for 2½ months. In four weeks she lost the possibility of reading, writing and knitting. . . . From the very moment Zygmunt told Lillan that he would leave her and the baby. So, the two doctors told me, that that moment our Lillan was ill and became slowly worse and worse from July 1962 until her death on April 28, 1963.*

In January 1964, Marjorie responded to Sophie with her thoughts on those several months with Marie-Louise:

I shared with Marie-Louise her hopes and disappointments and the many tensions arising from the divorce and from the birth Alex to such an extent have thought of her as a younger sister and felt all the matters deeply myself. Her tragic sickness and death came as a very great shock and sadness to me. I think of her often and pray for her daily.

It was a comfort to me that she and Alex were with me when my husband [Goossens] *died. Although we did not live together, I adored him and was grateful to him for his kindness and devotion. HE HAD BEEN VERY SICK FOR SOME TIME AND PLANNED A TRIP TO THE STATES WITH HIS NURSE WHEN ML WAS THERE, BUT HE DIED BEFORE THE TRIP. We were all most upset about his prospective arrival because of ML and Alex, but they could have stayed with friends of mine while he was here (for I could not refuse to have any dying husband and it would have been worked out so that everyone was taken care of).*

I go into some detail because I want you to understand the difficulties of my situation and conflict of loyalties at that time and that I was doing the best I could for them all. "Best" was not always satisfactory, no one could be [more] sorrowful than I am. My own health was not too strong at the time and sometimes I was sick, too.

Despite all the sorrow this whole affair has caused me, I am very glad that I had the chance to know ML and to be her friend. She was sweet and often a child, and the harsh realities of life were too much for her.

On February 16, 1964, Sophie wrote to Marjorie: *"Zigmunt tells me that you would be willing to take dear Alexander if something happens here. At my age one must be prepared to leave this world and . . . I am very thankful that I may think of him in your care. He is a little American boy, and I am going to ask the lawyer to give me his passport."*

Although there were many nannies, Sophie kept Alexander until he was six years old before he went to live with his father in Munich.

In the summers of 1961–62, members of outstanding families from four countries—Germany, Poland, the United Kingdom, and America—rendezvoused in a sleepy Pennsylvania village. A world-famous conductor had come to arrange a divorce. Thanks to Marjorie, a countess, the stepdaughter of the last Queen of Portugal, and a Polish ambassador's son had found a safe haven for the birth of their son and their marriage.

CHAPTER 10

After the Storm

Initially comfortable with the grandmother raising his young son, Ziggy visited often and took the child on numerous vacations. In 1964, Marjorie made her delayed trip to Europe and spent four days visiting Ziggy and Alexander and meeting Sophie.[1]

On more than one occasion, while Ziggy visited, Sophie, protective of Alexander and blaming Ziggy for her daughter's death, shouted at Ziggy that he was a "*murderer.*"

Sophie passed away in 1971 at age eighty-seven, having stayed in touch with Marjorie by letters for all those years.

Alexander and his father returned to visit Marjorie in Landisburg in 1970. While only eight years old, Alexander remembered the trip and his "aunt" decades later. As no letters have been discovered after 1971 between Ziggy and Marjorie, there was no information in the archives related to what became of the father and his child.

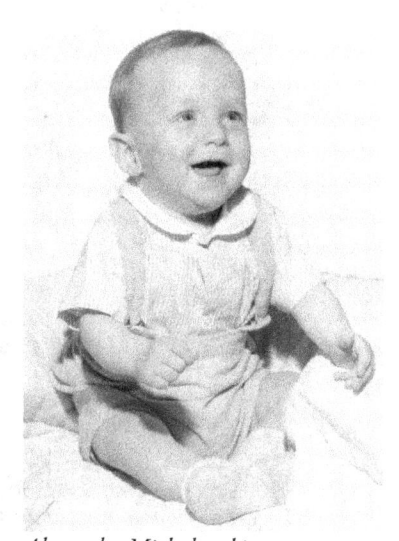

Alexander Michalowski at age two. MFG Archive.

Zygmunt, the Successful Cold Warrior

Ziggy, however, continued to climb the corporate ladder and became the director of Radio Free Europe's Polish Department before retirement in the early 1980s. During his career, he serialized Aleksandr Solzhenitsyn's three-volume *Gulag Archipelago* and presented it in its entirety on the radio in fifteen-minute segments.

In a letter to Solzhenitsyn, Ziggy said, "*It was our intention to reveal to the Polish people the communion of suffering which all the peoples subject to communist rule have been sharing in varying degrees.*" On at least one occasion, Ziggy lunched with a Catholic Polish bishop who later became Pope John Paul II.

Alexander remembers an American lady who moved in with them and lived several years as a "stepmother," teaching him English. That relationship dissolved, as did others. Alexander remarked that even in late old age, his father still surrounded himself with the young ladies.

Zygmunt Michalowski. Radio Free Europe.

Ziggy died at ninety-two on September 11, 2010, having been honored by the new Poland, shed of its communist past. He is buried in Kraków, the city of his birth and distinguished ancestors.[2]

Ziggy's son, Alexander, stands on the far left of the interment picture next to Ziggy's nephew, Philippe Ballaux. Alexander Michalowski identified the photograph in August 2021.

Marjorie Made a Final Life-Changing Decision

Throughout the 1960s and early 1970s, Marjorie continued to make Fetter House her home base, although she traveled often and spent months in the mid-1960s providing "music therapy" for mental patients at a clinic in Florida. Caring for her aged mother, Fannie, also consumed her days. She spent time with her mother in Palm Beach until the Florida house was sold. Fannie lived out her last years in her Carlisle home, where she was looked after by a caregiver. She died in 1975.

Marjorie in the 1960s.

Marjorie was restless and found her peaceful domicile in Pennsylvania confined. She entertained occasionally, employing a chef and butler for her dinner parties. She was a woman who was more comfortable in Europe and less so in the rural, heavily Protestant Pennsylvania countryside.

Dr. Joe Matunis's wife, Suzanne, remembered a visit by Marjorie, welcoming their Roman Catholic family to their new home in Perry County. When Suzanne opened the door, a tall, elegantly dressed woman stood there. Marjorie threw her head back and haughtily said, "*I am Lady Goossens, and you may as well not unpack your bags as you will not be accepted here as they (the locals) don't like Catholics.*" In a 2024 interview, Suzanne stated emphatically, "*We never had any problems. Everyone was very welcoming.*"[3]

Marjorie traveled annually to Europe, usually for retreats to her two Catholic convents in France. As the 1960s gave way to the 1970s, she spent months in Switzerland studying Jungian psychology to explore the meaning of her dreams. She kept a diary with information on her past, and the contents have been incorporated into this book.

Her mother's death further reduced Marjorie's ties with Pennsylvania. Marjorie's own health became an issue in 1965 when she was hospitalized in Carlisle for an undisclosed issue.

Ever the searcher for her life's purpose and spending increased time in the village of Saint-Mathieu-de-Tréviers in southern France, she made her final life-changing decision.[4]

Marjorie Moved to France

Marjorie decided on a new, don't-look-back direction for her life. On December 31, 1974, she deeded Fetter House to the Historical Society of Perry County. She left her furniture, family papers, school records, memorabilia, and hundreds of letters from the 1950s and 1960s.

She moved to a house she built adjacent to the Dominican convent in Saint-Mathieu-de-Tréviers, a small village north of Montpellier. For a year or so after her relocation to France, she provided musical therapy at a mental health sanatorium before lung issues forced her into retirement.

In the early 1980s, she stayed in touch with the Historical Society, the owners of Fetter House, and agreed to pay $1,945 to recondition her grand piano in early 1985. She was not above criticizing the Society when it published a leaflet she felt was badly written and pretentious when it described Fetter House as a mansion.

In 1985, she traveled to Zurich to stay with a friend. She wrote that her feet were deformed with arthritis and that she had shingles. There were also serious lung issues. By 1986, she tired easily but still traveled to Normandy to visit friends. In March 1987, she replied to her

Pennsylvania attorney, George Faller, Jr., that she could not have house guests. That month, she had only been to the convent once for Mass and lunch. A doctor wanted her to walk more, but she found it boring. She preferred to watch sports on television.

Faller managed her American investments and taxes. Her net worth in 1985 dollars amounted to $1.8 million, and she was in the 48% tax bracket. She annually donated to the convent and $10,000 to Carlisle charities. In 1988, she had a driver take her to Normandy, which was probably her last visit. In 1989, she wrote that she missed her country and her friends but had no strength to visit. In a 1990 letter, the last correspondence in her archive, she wrote that George should not give up on her as a client, as he was considering retirement, because she was dependent on him.

When the authors contacted the convent in 2021, a few of the older nuns said they remembered Marjorie only as an elderly lady. Little did they realize the amazing life Marjorie had lived.[5]

Marjorie's home, adjacent to the convent of the Dominicans of Sainte-Marie des Tourelles in the village of Saint-Mathieu-de-Tréviers, France. Alexander Michalowski, 2021.

Marjorie died on October 18, 2000. Born in rural Pennsylvania, the woman who searched for meaning in life rests in the convent cemetery in southern France, far from Fetter House in Pennsylvania. In her will, she left sizeable sums to two of her stepdaughters, Anne, $20,000, from Eugene's first marriage, and Doni, $10,000, from Eugene's second marriage.

The rest of Marjorie's estate went to three organizations: the largest, including her house, to the convent. The remainder, she divided equally between endowment for Fetter House and the Carlisle Area Health and Wellness Medical Foundation.[6]

Restless, Reckless, and Redemption

How does one grasp the enormity and variables of Marjorie's twentieth-century life? Was she just an adventuress laden with desire, or was she a bright woman frustrated not to find a role other than wife and mistress? Was Ziggy correct in urging her to take employment and cease being selfish? Halfway through her life, did she not find peace in the Roman Catholic Church and achieve mastery in medieval music?

Restless would be the word to define the period from her first marriage in 1932 to her third with Eugene Goossens in 1946 and their first years in Australia.

Yet, by 1952, her marriage with Eugene had soured, culminating in her dramatic departure from Australia with Ziggy. This action was reckless, leaving behind a whiff of scandal as she separated herself almost entirely from Goossens and her stepdaughters who had bonded with her. For a few months in 1954, she returned to Australia for Doni's wedding but left her Australian home not long afterward. Her "abandoning" Renee in a stern Catholic French boarding school at age fifteen seems callous.

As her romantic passions lessened in her late forties, especially with Ziggy, she returned to Pennsylvania and invested her life in studying medieval religious music. In 1959, she took holy orders to become a third-degree secular nun, turning her life to spiritual contemplation. She often went on spiritual retreats in the States and France.

Redemption is found in her kindness to Marie-Louise Douglas; her empathy toward the distressed countess's mother, Sophie Douglas, in Germany; and her concern for Alexander. Later, in the 1960s, she provided musical therapy for the mentally disturbed in a Florida clinic.

Upon her relocation to France in the mid-1970s, she provided her services at a mental health sanatorium before her health began to fail. No doubt her musical talent and expertise provided inspirational music on many occasions for convent worship services. The final decades of her life were surrounded by prayer and music.

After decades of searching, Marjorie had let go of her earlier travails and passions and embraced the remainder of her time in contemplation and the gentle ritual of the Roman Catholic Church. Hopefully, as she aged and her health failed, peace and spiritual love enveloped the last quarter century of her eventful life.

Over the decades, she refused to give interviews to reporters or historians regarding her time in Australia or her marriage to Eugene. Why did she leave behind her memorabilia, letters, furniture, books, and beloved grand piano, and move to France, never to return to reclaim them?

Perry County commissioner and local historian Gary Eby has puzzled over why she left her memorabilia in Fetter House. He believes she left it all behind on purpose, waiting to be discovered to tell the story of her adventurous and complicated life. Perhaps she did so to bear testimony to life's passions, reminding all of our humanity and search for love and meaning. If so, let this be her story, and let us learn from it and ponder.

Marjorie's final resting place in the cemetery of her beloved convent in France. Photograph by Alexander Michalowski, 2021.

EPILOGUE

Finding Alexander and How the Book Came to Be

During the authors' research, we wondered what happened to Alexander, the boy child of Ziggy and Marie-Louise. While Marjorie left her letters and memorabilia in 1974 at Fetter House, never to retrieve them, the only letters saved after this date were those her attorney retained at his Carlisle office.

With additional exploration, we found that Ziggy died in 2010 at age ninety-two in Kraków, Poland. In a web photograph was his coffin with several men standing by the bier. Could one of these persons be Ziggy's son?

In September 2020, we wrote a letter to the Lake Constance, Germany, castle of the Douglas family, inquiring if an Alexander Michalowski lived in the family home. There was no answer until an email arrived in April 2021 from Alexander himself, living in Munich, Germany. The letter had been forwarded belatedly from the castle office, still owned by a branch of the family.

Emails flew back and forth, and, in August 2021, vaccinated for COVID protection, the authors flew to France to rendezvous with Alexander. We sought to learn more about his father and his relationship with Marjorie. The place selected for our conference was the one-thousand-year-old, impressive Château de Chargé, now a hotel and conference center near Richelieu in central France.

The Château was owned by Alexander's cousin, Philippe Ballaux, and his wife, Nadine. Philippe is Ziggy's sister's son and attended Ziggy's

The Château de Chargé, Razines, France.

funeral. The couple was most hospitable, and Philippe added his memories of family to our research. His chef, Martin, with his fantastic dishes, added, along with his French wine selections, to our waistlines.

It proved to be an ideal place to spread out our various materials in the conference room, where we spent six busy days reviewing with Alexander, examining books and an important family document. The document was a sixty-page unpublished manuscript by Alexander's grandmother, Maria Czarnomska Wodzicka Michalowski (1886–1979), which detailed her long life from czarist Russia to the Cold War. Of particular interest were descriptions of Ziggy's father's activities as second secretary at the Austrian-Hungarian Dual Monarchy embassy in Belgrade in July 1914 when war broke out between Serbia and the Hapsburg Empire.

Alexander's memories of his father and family proved a gold mine of information, fleshing out our story of Marjorie and adding layers of history to our understanding of two families whose lives spanned a century of war and revolution in Europe.

Preserving the stories of the four principal characters in this book, plus a supporting cast of memorable persons, has proved a fascinating endeavor; hence, this work articulating these remarkable stories.

However, time and space do not allow us to engage in writing the rich tapestry of Ziggy's and Marie-Louise's ancestorial stories. Regretfully,

Barbara Holliman, Philippe Ballaux (in a Perry County, Pennsylvania, bicentennial shirt), and Ziggy and Marie-Louise's son, Alexander Michalowski, at lunch in France.

they are too large for inclusion in this tome and too ambitious a task for this couple. We thank Alexander for his input and for sharing amazing family stories. Hopefully, a European historian will gather threads from this work and produce a book worthy of the tale.

How the Book Came to Be

This deep exploration into the lives of Marjorie, Eugene, Ziggy, and Marie-Louise was made possible because Marjorie left hundreds of letters, photographs, and diaries in Landisburg, Pennsylvania.

In 2018, while board president of the Historical Society of Perry County and a trained historian, Glenn, along with Barbara, discovered the material scattered in drawers, boxes, and trucks, uncatalogued but preserved for almost half a century. At that time, the Society also received Marjorie's remaining correspondence from the attorney of the trust established at her death in 2000.

We thought it best to collect and inventory the materials for preservation purposes. As we began to put items in chronological order, we discovered the bulk of letters were from two men.

One group was written by Marjorie's third husband, Eugene, from 1953 to 1962. A second collection was from her Polish lover, Ziggy, a major figure in Marjorie's life. These were written between 1952 and 1971. Our research led us into the complex and fascinating life of yet another person, one Countess Marie-Louise Douglas Michalowski, whose tragic story lay hidden away for decades in Marjorie's trunks and the memories of her only child, Alexander Michalowski, a citizen of Germany and, due to his birthplace, the United States.

This is not a study of Goossens's musical talents but rather his life as Marjorie's husband, the tragic collapse of his career due to an affair with a "witch," and his broken last years. For the first time, the letters and cablegrams Goossens sent Marjorie from Australia during his humiliating spring of 1956 are herein revealed and available to historians. They provide a stunning insight into his tortured feelings and a scandal that still echoes across the decades in Australian cultural and social history.

Building a timeline of Marjorie's life through letters, diaries, calendars, passports, and photographs, we found a complex woman who had traveled widely, loved deeply and often, and, eventually, found spiritual

Fetter House today in Landisburg, Pennsylvania. Preserved by the Historical Society of Perry County with an endowment provided by Lady Marjorie Fetter Goossens. Open by appointment.

peace in a Catholic convent in southern France. Her travels alone, several of which we recorded in detail, yield fascinating insight to the complexity and difficulty of global journeys after World War II before the arrival of jet airplanes.

In 2019, Barbara constructed a PowerPoint presentation of Marjorie's life and began showing it to local groups for charity. Without exception, all who viewed the story were amazed, and sometimes disturbed, by Marjorie's journey and her eventually finding peace through her music and religious faith.

When we started our research, little did we imagine we would be undertaking an investigation that would reveal the incredible lives of persons in America, Australia, and Europe coping with disaster, war, love, tragedy, recovery, and reconciliation in the twentieth century. The letters and memorabilia, now collected, digitalized, and arranged for future historians, remain at Fetter House under the stewardship of the History Society of Perry County, where Marjorie left them decades ago.

Glenn N. and Barbara L. Holliman, Newport, Pennsylvania
glennhistory@gmail.com

Endnotes

Chapter 1: Marjorie's Early Life and Loves

1. Photos and memorabilia, Marjorie Fetter Goossens (MFG) Archive, Historical Society of Perry County (HSPC), Fetter House, Landisburg, Pennsylvania. Letters and photographs have been digitally stored.

2. PA 46379 Death Certificate, Dorthey Jane Fetter, August 18, 1916–May 26, 1921.

3. *Carlisle Evening Herald,* June 17, 1918.

4. MFG to attorney George Faller Jr., 1983 (no month or day provided).

5. MFG scrapbook, MFG Archive.

6. Telephone interview by Barbara Holliman with Juilliard College archive director, Juilliard College, New York, New York, February 20, 2019.

7. Court of Common Pleas, Cumberland County, May 1935; Wedding invitation, MFG Archive.

8. Carlisle Sentinel, June 11, 1936.

9. Philadelphia Inquirer, April 11, 1943.

10. Reno, Nevada, divorce decree, MFG Archive. Reno Gazette, December 14, 1944. US Department of Veterans Affairs, Death File BIRLS 1850-2010, Veterans Administration, June 26, 1950. Philadelphia Inquirer obituary, January 2, 1979.

11. Carole Rosen, The Goossens (Boston: Northeastern University Press, 1993), 247. The Goossens is a comprehensive biography of Eugene and his siblings. Cincinnati Enquirer, October 23, 1943. Birthday card, MGF Archive.

12. Atlanta Journal, March 15, 1942; Cincinnati Enquirer, October 8 and 10, 1942; Boston Globe, December 29, 1944.

13. Rosen, 62, 65, 71, 95–109, 142–159, 242–247. Historians are indebted to the author who interviewed and recorded numerous members and friends of the Goossens family and had access to Eugene's letters to persons other than Marjorie. While there are numerous articles written on EG's first two marriages and work in Rochester and Cincinnati, here one will find it all capsuled into one volume. There is information on MFG, but a few items are incorrect, as she never gave interviews to the press or historians after the March 1955 telephone call from the Sydney Sun, when she was informed of her husband's arrest. Cincinnati Post, May 13, 1946. Front page article on EG and MFG "secret wedding."

14. Correspondence between the women continued for decades. Marjorie left Doni $10,000 in her will. MFG Archive.

Chapter 2: Third Time a Charm?

1. Rosen, 261, 262.

2. MFG diary, 1946 entry, MFG Archive; Rosen, 243.
3. Cincinnati Post, May 13, 1946.
4. MFG diary, May 1946.
5. EG diary, 1946; MFG diary, 1946, MFG Archive.
6. Rosen. Over five hundred pages of in-depth coverage of Eugene III and his talented, accomplished siblings.
7. MFG 1946 diaries, MFG Archive.
8. Rosen, 273.
9. MFG diary, June 4, 1947, MFG Archive.
10. MFG 1947-48 diaries, MFG Archive; The Sun, July 6, 1947.
11. Rosen, 290; Renee Goossens, Belonging (ABC Publishing, 2003), 4, 87.
12. ABC Weekly, November 1, 1947.
13. Tucker, Harold, Rewind: The Sad Tale of Sir Eugene Goossens, edited by Michael Cathcart, ABC documentary, September 5, 2004.
14. MFG draft letter to a friend, March 1950, MFG Archive.
15. MFG 1949–1952 diaries, MFG Archive.
16. Carlisle Sentinel, May 1950; The Sun, NSW Australia, May 18, 1950; Frederic Raphael, Somerset Maugham and His World (Heinemann Publishing: London, 1922), 54.
17. MFG diary, 1950, MFG Archive.
18. MFG diary, 1969, MFG Archive.
19. Personal interview, Glenn N. Holliman with Anne M. Taylor, September 2023.
20. MFG 1952 diary, MFG Archive.
21. Shelia Wayne, transcriber of MFG diaries, 1952–53.
22. The Daily Telegraph, Sydney, Australia, April 4, 1953.
23. MFG diary, 1952, MFG Archive.
24. Rosen, 340.
25. Nevill Dury, "Norton, Rosaleen Miriam (1917-1979)," 40-41. National Center of Biography, Australian National University.

Chapter 3: Ziggy Enters Marjorie's Restless, Reckless Life

1. ZM to MFG, November 4, 1952, MFG Archive. There are dozens of letters from ZM to MFG between 1952 and 1971. These letters through 1971 can be found in the MFG archive in 8x11" envelopes by year. There are challenges, as some letters were without envelopes with postmarks or just the day, not date, month, or year, at the top of page one. All letters also in digital format.
2. Interview, Glenn and Barbara Holliman with Alexander Michalowski, son of Ziggy, August 2021.
3. Résumé of Zygmunt Michalowski provided by his son, Alexander Michalowski. Alexander's personal insights were provided in interviews over six days in August 2021.
4. The Telegraph, Sydney, Australia, April 4, 1953.
5. Truth, January 3, 1954; (Sydney) Sun, February 14, 1954; New Castle (Australia) Morning News, March 22, 1954, MFG Archive
6. MFG diary, 1953, MFG Archive; ZM to MFG, MFG Archive; Alexander Michalowski interview with the Hollimans, August 2021.

Chapter 4: Separation and Eugene's Knighthoo

1. Goossens, 67–69.
2. EG to MFG, March 8, 1954, MFG Archive. Tucker, The Sad Tale of Sir Eugene Goossens. Interviews by Michelle Arrow and Michael Cathcart with Pamela Main, Renee Goossens, Sidonie Goossens (Eugene's sister), and police detective Bert Trevenar of the Sydney, New South Wales, Police Department, September 5, 2004.
3. EG to MFG, January 8, 1955, MFG Archive.
4. Goossens, 76–84, 97–107.
5. Reverend Dr. John Thompson to MFG, August 31, 1955; October 19 and 22, 1955; January 20, 1956; MFG Archive.
6. Goossens, 198–238.
7. Sydney Morning Herald, March 13, 1955.
8. EG to MFG, May 1955, MFG Archive.
9. Sydney Morning Herald, June 9, 1955.
10. Texas Telegram, March 13, 1955.

Chapter 5: The Conductor's Fatal Attraction

1. Rosen, 339; David Salter, "The Conservatorium Director and the Witch," The Sydney Morning Herald, originally published in Good Weekend, July 3, 1999.
2. Harold Tucker, The Sad Tale of Sir Eugene Goossens.
3. Ibid.; Rosen, 349.
4. Photographic collection, MFG Archive.
5. The Age, December 25, 1955.

Chapter 6: The Day the Music Stopped

1. "The Conservatorium Director and the Witch," Good Weekend, July 4, 1999. The Fall of the House, Australian Film Commission, 2002. Geoffrey Morehouse, Sydney (New York: Harcourt, 1997), 166–171. Tucker, The Sad Tale of Sir Eugene Goossen.
2. Sydney Morning Herald, March 23, 1956.
3. EG to MFG, March–May 1956, MFG Archive.
4. Sydney Morning Herald, April 1956.
5. EG to MFG, April 18, 1956, MFG Archive.
6. EG to MFG, April 24, 1956, MFG Archive.

Chapter 7: The Aftermath of Scandal

1. *The Age,* May 30, 1956.
2. EG to MFG, July 1956, MFG Archive.
3. ZM to MFG, fall 1956, MFG Archive.
4. MFG to EG, February 1957, MFG Archive.
5. Harold Tucker, The Sad Tale of Sir Eugene Goossens.
6. MFG to ZM, February 1957, MFG Archive.
7. ZM to MFG, June 17, 1957, MFG Archive.
8. MFG diary, 1957, MFG Archive.

9. ZM to MFG, March 1957, MFG Archive.
10. MFG diary, 1957, MFG Archive.
11. Jacqueline Sills to MFG, May 3, 1957, MFG Archive.
12. Memorabilia of diplomas and papers, MFG Archive.
13. MFG diary, May 27, 1958, MFG Archive; MFG diaries, 1959 and 1960, MFG Archive.
14. MFG diary, 1959, MFG Archive.
15. EG to MFG, July 1959, MFG Archive.
16. MFG diary, 1959, MFG Archive.
17. MFG becomes Novitate in the third order of Domincans, sulare. Letter from White Sisters, Franklin, PA, MFG Archive.
18. Renee Goossens's numerous letters to MFG and MFG's replies, 1957–1961, MFG Archive.
19. Tucker interview, 2004.
20. Sydney Morning Herald, July 3, 1999.

Chapter 8: The Death of Goossens
1. EG to MFG, August 1961, MFG Archive.
2. EG to MFG, June 1962, MFG Archive.
3. PM to MFG, January–July 1962, MFG Archive.
4. David Salter, "The Conservatorium and the Witch."
5. Sidonie Goossens to MFG, MFG Archive.
6. Sydney Morning Herald, May 22, 1993.

Chapter 9: A Countess Comes to Fetter House
1. ZM to MFG, November 1961, MFG Archive.
2. ZM to MFG, November 1961, MFG Archive. AM interview with the Hollimans, August 2021.
3. Sophie Douglas to MFG, March 14, 1962, MFG Archive.
4. ZM to MFG; Marie-Louise Douglas Michalowski to MFG, August 1962–January 1963.
5. SD to MFG, February 1962, MFG Archive.
6. Tacoma Daily Ledger and Tacoma News Tribune, May 12, 1906. Winsor Star, October 21, 1938. MFG to SD, January 1963, MFG Archie.
7. ZM to MFG, May 1, 1963; Alexander Michalowski interview with the Hollimans, August 2001.
8. ZM to MFG, June 1963, MFG Archive.

Chapter 10: After the Storm
1. Passports and diaries, MFG Archive.
2. AM interview, August 2021.
3. Suzanne Matunis interview with Barbara Holliman, 2023; Marianne Flowers, friend of MFG who dined at Fetter House on at least one occasion, interview, 2019.
4. Passports and memorabilia, MFG Archive. Carlisle Sentinel, Fannie Fetter's obit-

uary, October 1975. Letters from Switzerland friends. Unidentified nun of Sainte-Marie des Tourelles in the village of Saint-Mathieu-de-Tréviers, 2021. Carlisle Sentinel, November 23, 1965.

5. Letters to her attorney, MFG Archive.
6. Death certificate and will, MFG Archive.

Abbreviations

MFG	Marjorie Fetter Goossens
EG	Eugene A. Goossens III
ZM	Zygmunt Michalowski
AM	Alexander Michalowski
ML	Countess Marie-Louise Douglas Michalowski
SD	Countess Sophie Douglas
PM	Pamela Main
ACISS	Australian Counsel for Societal Settlement

Acknowledgments and Bibliography

Drury, Nevill. "Notron, Rosaleen Miriam (1917-1979)," National Centre of Biography, Australian National University.

Goossens, Eugene III. *Overtures and Beginners*. Methuen Press: London, 1952.

Eugene's autobiography of his musical career. He scarcely mentions any family members.

Goossens, Renee. *Belonging.* , 2003. Sydney, Australian Broadcasting Company, 2003

The engaging, often bitter-sweet memoirs of Goossen's youngest child. A few memories, while heartfelt, are not supported by later research.

Johnson, Marguerite. *The-Witching-Hour-Sex-Magic-in-1950s-Australia*. https://www.scribd.com/document/84636594/ (An exploration of Goossens and other artists' fascination with the occult.)

Juilliard School of Music, Alumni office, New York, New York (MFG attended January-May 1931).

Marjorie Fetter Goossens Archive. Fetter House, Landisburg, Pennsylvania, Historical Society of Perry County, Pennsylvania.

Moorhouse, Geoffrey. *Sydney, The Story of a City*. Harcourt: New York, 1997.

Raphael, Frederic. *Somerset Maugham and his World*. London: Book Club Associates, 1978.

Rosen, Carole. *The Goossens, A Musical Century*. Boston: Northeastern University Press, 1993.

Comprehensive, excellent and invaluable work based on interviews and correspondence of Goossen family members and friends.

Salter, David. https://www.smh.com.au/lifestyle/the-conservatorium-director-and-the-witch-20150702-gi3h8y.html; Originally published in *Good Weekend*, July 3, 1999, updated 2015. A detailed and comprehensive description of the arrest and trial of Australia's classical conductor Eugene A. Goossens III due to his relationship with Rosalee Norton, a self-anointed witch.

Tucker, Harold. *The Sad Tale of Sir Eugene Goossens*. Edited by Michael Cathcart, ABC, 2004. This includes interviews by Michelle Arrow with Pamela Main, Renee Goossens, Doni Goossens, and Bert Trevenar.

Wayne, Shelia, Shorthand Interpreter, Wayne Communications. Avon Lake, Ohio: August 2020.

Weekly, Australian Broadcasting Company, 1947 magazine.

Index

Alinda, Pennsylvania, 2
Aplvor, Denis, 48
Apocalypse, The (Goossen's composition), 44, 45, 47
Arden, Elizabeth, 24, 65
Auckland, New Zealand, 16
Australia Broadcasting Corporation, 13, 17, 56, 60, 78
Australian Council of International Societal Services (ACISS), 24, 27

Baldwin's, School, 4
Ballaux, Nadine, 94
Ballaux, Philippe, 88, 94, 96
Beecham, Thomas, 9, 47
Bennelong Point (Australia), 18–19
Bernstein, Leonard, 13
Blauth, Christopher 'Kit', 67–68
Bonynge, Richard, 74
Bryn Mawr, Pennsylvania, 4, 5

Carlisle, Pennsylvania, 2–4, 7, 24, 41, 69, 79, 81, 89, 91–92
Chateau de Charge, Richelieu, France, 94–95
Cincinnati Symphony Orchestra, 11
  May Festival, 12
Colonnade Hotel, 44, 46, 64–67
Composers Concourse, 48
Craig, Nathanial, 50, 51
Cubit, Dorothy, 16

Dickinson College, 5
  Law school, 7
Douglas, Augusta Victoria, deposed Queen of Portugal, widow of King Manual II, 82, 86
Douglas, Count Robert, 79, 81–82
Douglas, Countess Sophie, 81–87, 92

Eastman School of Music, 9
Eby, Gary, 93
Elizabeth II (Queen), 46, 50

Emery, Arthur B, 6
Epiphany, Soisy-sur-Seine (convent in France), 41–42, 57, 71–72

Faller, George, Jr. 91
Fetter, Dorthey, 1–2
Fetter, Fannie Rhinesmith, 2–4, 7, 34, 56–57, 89
Fetter, Henry, 1
Fetter House, 1, 2, 4, 5, 52, 68–69, 75, 79, 81, 83, 90–94, 97–98
Fetter, William J., 1–4, 7, 34, 68, 82–83
Foulkrod, Irungard Bellingradt, 8
Foulkrod, John Jacob III, 6–8. 11, 25
Fountains, The, 41
Fry, Christopher, 71

Galicia, Podolia, 30
Goossens, Anne, 10, 16, 92
Goossens, Connie, 39
Goossens, Eugene Ansley, Jr., 13
Goossens, Eugene Ansley, III, 2
  Meeting MFG, 9–10
  Marriage MFG, 12–15
  Travel and Australia, 16–22
  Norton, Roseleen, 26
  Marriage troubles, 32–37
  Doni's wedding, 38
  Letter to MFG, 39–40
  Renee's issues, 42
  Knighthood, 43–44
  Norton Coven, 45–46
  European Trip, 47–50
  Arrest at Mascot, 50
  Scandal, 51–64
  Disgrace, 76 Hamilton Terrace, London, 65–68
  Decline, Death and Recognition, 70–78, 83, 92–93, 96–97
Goossens, Jane, 10, 76–77
Goossens, Julia, 10, 76
Goossens, Leon, 13, 41, 72

Goossens, Marie, 13
Goossens, Marjorie Fetter,
  Childhood, 2–4
  Education and piano, 5
  Marriages, 6–8
  Meeting EG, 9
  Marriage to EG, 12
  Travel, 15–17
  Australian success, 18, 20
  Opera House proposed, 19
  Wahroonga home, 20, 27
  Travel and the Pope, 20–21
  Marriage troubles, 22–23
  Travel to UN meeting and Carlisle, 24
  Thomas and shorthand diary, 25–26
  Meets Zygmunt Michalowski, 27–30
  Elopes with Zig, 31–37
  Doni's wedding, 38
  Returns to Europe, 39–40, 41–47
  Scandal, cablegrams and letters, 50, 52–60, 64
  Paris, Fetter House and Gregorian Chants, 65–70
  Return to Europe in1959, 71–72
  Renee, 73
  Divorce, not to be, 75–78
  Countess and her son, 79–87
  Move to France, death, 89–98
Goossens, Renee, 10–11, 14, 16–17, 20, 38
  Belonging, 39–44, 48, 57, 64–65, 68, 70, 72–73, 78, 92
Goossens, Sidonie (Doni, daughter of Eugene), 11, 14, 16–17, 20–22, 34, 37–39, 55–56, 72–73, 92
Goossens-Millar, Sidonie (sister of Eugene), 13, 45–46, 58, 72, 71
Graves, Robert, 71
Gray, E. (E. Goossens' fictious name), 64
Greenaway, physician, no first name, 56
Greenlees, Gavin, 45, 51

Heseltine, Philip, 45
Hill School, 6
Historical of Perry County, Pennsylvania, 1, 90, 96–97
Holliman, Barbara Long, 96, 98
Holliman, Glenn N., 94, 98
Holmes, Betty, 10

Imperial Airlines, 13

Indiana, University of, Jacob's School of Music, 69, 72
Inquirer, Philadelphia, 7

James, Bill, 62
John Paul II (Pope), 88
Juilliard (music), 5

Kings Cross (Australia), 45, 51, 62
Krakow, Poland, 30, 88
Krasicki, Dennis von Bieberstein, 80
Krasicki, Stas, 29
Krasicki, Xavery, 29

Lancaster Bomber, 13
Lafayette College, 2
Lake Constance, Germany, 80, 82–83, 94
Landisburg, Pennsylvania, 1, 52, 68, 70, 75, 81, 87, 96–97
Langenstein Castle (Germany), 80
Latona, Peter, 78
Lewis, Janet, EG's 2nd wife, 10–11, 16, 24, 73
Lloyd Triestino, 32
Loundes, 7 Place, London, 34

Maida Vale (England), 48, 61
Main, Pamela, 40, 64, 67, 73–78
Mary Manse College, Toledo, Ohio, 69
Matunis, Dr. Joe, 81
Matunis, Suzanne, 89
Maugham, Somerset (*East of Suez*), 20
Menzies, Robert (Prime Minister of Australia), 48
Michalowski, Alexander Douglas, 29, 30, 36, 79–83, 86–88, 91–97
Michalowski, Maria Wodzicka, 30, 95
Michalowski, Marie-Louise Douglas Bieberstein, 2, 79–85, 92, 94, 96–97
Michalowski, Zygmunt (son), 27–35
  advice to MFG, 36–37, 65, 67–71
  wife and son, 79–88, 92, 94–97

Michalowski, Zygmunt (father), 29
Millar, Dorothy "Boonie" Smith-Dodsworth, 10, 16, 75
Morning News, Sydney, 39
Morris, Joe, 46, 51
Moses, Charles, 14, 55–57
Mount Holyoke College, 5
Murray, A.G., 72

New South Wales Music Conservatory (Australia), 14, 26, 50, 52, 56
Nice, France, 21, 60–62, 64, 70, 79
Northcott, Sir John, 19
Norton, Rosaleen, 26, 40, 44–46, 51, 54, 78

Oakes (unknown first name; real estate agent), 58
Overtures and Beginnings, 15

Palm Beach, Florida, 2, 12, 56, 69, 89
Paris, France, 25, 33–34, 41, 44, 48, 50, 52, 57, 65–66, 71, 76, 83
Paris, Kentucky, 13
Parry (fictional character), 61–62
Perry County, Pennsylvania, 1, 2, 68, 79, 89–90, 93, 96, 97–98
Pius XII (Pope), 21
Plaza Hotel, NYC, 24
Port Towsend (ship), 39
Post, Cincinnati, 13
Princeton, 6, 7, 25

Queen Mary (ship), 13

Radio Free Europe, 30, 36, 70, 87–88
RCA Victor, 8–9, 65
Redgrave, Rachel, 25
Reine, Fritz, 12
Rochester Philharmonic Orchestra, 9
Royal Hawaiian Hotel, 15
Royal Philharmonic, 45, 48
Royal Symphony Orchestra, 47
Rosens, Carole, 8, 22

Saint-Mathieu-de-Tréviers, Convent of Dominicans of Sainte-Marie des Tourelles, 60, 64, 90–91
Savage Club, London, 50, 61–62
Scott, Cyril, 45
Seven Stars Garage, 3
Shand, Jack, 54–55
Solzhenitsyn, Alexsandr, 30, 88
Stratyn, Ukraine, 29
Sutherland, Joan, 74
Sydney Symphony Orchestra (Australia), 13–14, 16, 46, 50, 52
Sydney Opera House, 73, 77–78
Symphonette Society, Philadelphia, 7

Taylor, Anne M., 22
Thomas (unknown last name), 23, 25–26, 28, 33
Thompson, John, 41–42, 64, 70, 72
Tiley, Richard, 38
Trevenar, Bert, 50–51

Ultimo, Sydney, 78

Vancouver, 15–16
Van Wyck, Wilfred, 56, 73
Villa Douglas (Germany), 83

Wahroonga (Australia), 20, 27, 38–39
Walton, Ron, 50
Wargren, Albert (valet), 20
Wynnewood (Pennsylvania), 7–8, 11, 20

Young, John, 37, 64

Zurich, Switzerland, 90

About the Authors

Husband and wife, Glenn N. and Barbara L. Holliman of Newport, Pennsylvania, teamed together to research and write this intriguing story of another couple, Eugene A. Goossens III and Marjorie Fetter Goossens. This is the second book on which the Holliman's have collaborated, the first being *With Generous Hearts* based on their careers in philanthropy.

They discovered memorabilia, letters, photographs, and diaries in Marjorie's historic home, Fetter House in Landisburg near their own residence in Perry County, Pennsylvania. The two, who live not far from Fetter, reconstructed her life. This appealed to them as Glenn is a historian and Barb felt a passion to share this woman's story by embarking on a multi-year adventure piecing together the lives of this couple and other major persons in Marjorie's life.

Glenn, a former history teacher and independent school administrator, has a B.S. and M.A. in American History and an M.Ed. from Tennessee universities. He has served as president of the Pennsylvania Heritage Foundation, the 501(c)(3) for the State Museum and Archive and is active in multiple heritage preservation projects in Perry County, Pennsylvania.

Barb, former teacher, holds a B.S. and M.Ed. in art from Michigan and New York schools.

In 1988, the two formed Holliman Associates, a capital campaign fundraising firm that during their careers raised over one hundred million dollars for Episcopal parishes and dioceses in forty-eight states, the District of Columbia, the American Cathedral in Paris, and other not for profit agencies. In 2005, the firm was absorbed by the national Episcopal Church Foundation in New York. In 2009, the Hollimans retired and began volunteer work in Pennsylvania. Barb has remodeled and enlarged their 1870s farmhouse several times which is located in the Appalachian Ridge and Valley section of the Juniata River Valley. The couple enjoys their grandchildren and traveling numerous times to Europe.